SpeakEasy Spanish™

SURVIVAL SPANISH FOR RESTAURANTS AND HOTELS

Myelita Melton, MA

SpeakEasy Communications, Incorporated

Survival Spanish for Restaurants and Hotels

Author: Myelita A. Melton, MA
Cover illustration: Ellen Wass Beckerman
Published by SpeakEasy Communications, Inc.
116 Sea Trail Drive
Mooresville, NC 28117-8493
USA

ISBN: 978-0-978-69984-0

©2006 SpeakEasy Communications, Incorporated. All rights reserved.
No part of this guide may be duplicated or reproduced, stored in a retrieval system, or transmitted, in any form or by any means, electronic, mechanical, recording, or otherwise, without the express written consent of the author.

Survival Spanish for Restaurants and Hotels, SpeakEasy Spanish, SpeakEasy's Survival Spanish, SpeakEasy's Survival Spanish for Restaurants and Hotels, and SpeakEasySpanish.com are either trademarks or registered trademarks of SpeakEasy Communications, Inc. in the United States and/or other countries.

The content of this book is furnished for informational use only, is subject to change without notice, and should not be construed as a commitment by SpeakEasy Communications, Incorporated. SpeakEasy Communications, Incorporated assumes no responsibility or liability for any errors, omissions, or inaccuracies that may appear in the informational content contained in this guide.

Survival Spanish for Restaurants and Hotels
Table of Contents

USING THIS MATERIAL	1
SPEAKEASY'S SECRETS TO LEARNING SPANISH	2
AMIGOS SIMILARES Y FAMILIARES	5
THE SOUNDS OF SPANISH	5
THE SPANISH ALPHABET	7
THE FOUR "EXTRA" LETTERS	7
THE SPANISH ACCENT	8
PRONOUNCING SPANISH WORDS	9
SPANISH PUNCTUATION MARKS	9
SPANGLISH	10
MORE AMIGOS FAMILIARES	11
MUCHOS WAYS TO "PRACTICAR"	12
SPEAKEASY'S TIPS AND TECHNIQUES FOR COMUNICACIÓN	13
BEGINNING WORDS AND PHRASES	14
SPANISH SOUNDS RÁPIDO — WHAT DO I DO NOW?	15
CONVERSATIONS TO PRACTICE	16
¿CUÁL ES SU NOMBRE COMPLETO?	17
SPANISH NOUNS	18

A WORD ABOUT ADJECTIVES	**19**
COMMON ADJECTIVES — ADJETIVOS COMUNES	**20**
THE ESSENTIALS OF SPANISH VERBS	**21**
¡ACCIÓN!	**22**
THE SWEET SIXTEEN VERBS	**23**
IRREGULAR VERBS: THE BIG FIVE	**25**
ARE YOU HUNGRY? — ¿TIENE HAMBRE?	**27**
WHAT'S THE WEATHER? — ¿QUÉ TIEMPO HACE?	**28**
SPECIAL USES OF SER AND ESTAR	**29**
THE NUMBERS — LOS NÚMEROS	**31**
THE DAYS OF THE WEEK AND MONTHS OF THE YEAR	**34**
PRACTICING NUMBERS & DATES	**35**
WHAT TIME IS IT? — ¿QUÉ HORA ES?	**36**
SCHEDULING AN APPOINTMENT	**37**
THE QUESTIONS EVERYONE SHOULD KNOW	**38**
GETTING THE INFORMACIÓN	**39**
THE FAMILY — LA FAMILIA	**42**
EMPLOYEE BENEFITS AND HUMAN RESOURCES	**44**
MOTIVATION AND EVALUATION	**46**
MEALS AND BEVERAGES	**48**

IN THE KITCHEN	50
ACTION IN THE RESTAURANT	55
KITCHEN MACHINES	56
I'M HUNGRY!	58
FRUITS	61
VEGETABLES	63
DAIRY AND EGG PRODUCTS	65
BREADS, PASTA, DESSERTS AND MORE	67
COOKING METHODS	69
FLAVORS AND INGREDIENTS	70
AT THE TABLE	72
MEASUREMENTS	75
RESTAURANT INSPECTIONS	76
CLEANING PRODUCTS	79
IN THE GUEST'S ROOM	82
TALKING WITH THE HOUSEKEEPING	84
AROUND THE HOTEL	86
GIVING DIRECTIONS	88
AROUND TOWN	90
LANDSCAPING & IRRIGATION	92

ONE FOR THE ROAD: PHRASES TO USE ANY TIME	**95**
TYPING IN SPANISH ON YOUR COMPUTER	**97**
PRACTICING WHAT YOU HAVE LEARNED	**99**
ABOUT THE AUTHOR	**103**

Using This Material

Survival Spanish for Restaurants and Hotels is designed for adults with no previous experience in the Spanish language. Through research and interviews with professionals in your field, we have developed this material as a practical guide to using Spanish on the job. Wherever possible, we have chosen to use the similarities between English and Spanish to facilitate your success.

Throughout the manual, you will find study tips and pronunciation guides that will help you to say the words correctly. In the guides, we have broken down the Spanish words for you by syllable, choosing English words that closely approximate the required Spanish sound. This method makes learning Spanish more accessible because it doesn't seem as foreign. When you see letters that are **BOLD** in the guide, say that part of the word the loudest. The bold capital letters will show you where the emphasis falls for that word.

At SpeakEasy Communications, we believe that *communication* is more important than *conjugation*, and that what you learn must be practical for what you do. We urge you to set realistic, practical goals. Make practice a regular part of your day and you will be surprised at the progress you make!

What's The Proper Term?
Both!

Latino/Latina: Anyone from Latin America who speaks Spanish as his or her native language. (Preferred)

Hispanic: Anyone who speaks Spanish as his or her native language and traces family origin to Spain.

Note: Don't assume that because a person speaks Spanish that they are Mexican. They could be from anywhere in Latin America

Latinos in the US come mainly from the following three areas:

1. Mexico
2. Central and South America
3. Puerto Rico

According to US Census:

1. There are over 46 million in the US who speak Spanish.
2. Hispanics are America's majority minority.
3. By 2050 Hispanics will make up at least 25% of the US population.
4. Over 18% of the nation's school-aged children are Latino.
5. In 2010 Latino buying power is expected to top 1 trillion dollars.
6. Approximately 43% of Latinos are limited in English proficiency.

Many Latinos from El Salvador, Honduras and Guatemala immigrated to America because of Hurricane Mitch in 1998.

SpeakEasy's Secrets to Learning Spanish

Congratulations on your decision to learn Spanish! This decision is one of the smartest choices you will ever make considering the increasing diversity in our country. It's definitely one you will never regret. You are now among a growing number of America's visionary leaders, who want to build more trusting relationships with Hispanic-Americans, the fastest growing segment of our nation's population.

Learning Spanish is going to open many doors for you, and it will affect you in ways you can't imagine. By learning Spanish, you will be able to work more efficiently and safely in almost every workplace in the nation. Since bilingual employees are currently in short supply nationwide, you will find increasing job opportunities in almost every profession. In addition, you will be able to build stronger relationships with Latinos you meet anywhere you go. There's also another added benefit: You are going to raise your communication skills to a whole new level.

As an adult, learning a new language requires a certain mind set. It takes time, patience and more than a little stubbornness. Think about it. You didn't learn English overnight. You began crying as an infant. That was your first attempt at communication. Later you uttered syllables. When you did, your parents thought you were the world's smartest child, and they rewarded you constantly. After a few years you began to make simple sentences. By the time you reached your first class in school, if you were like me, you couldn't stop talking. So, you can't expect to know everything about Spanish by studying it for only a few weeks. You must give Spanish time to sink in just like English did.

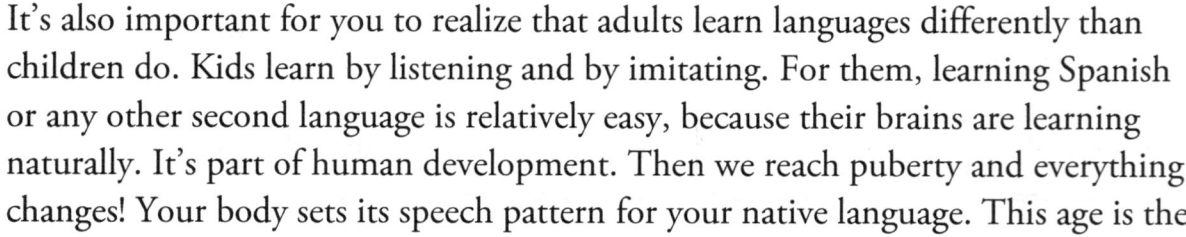

It's also important for you to realize that adults learn languages differently than children do. Kids learn by listening and by imitating. For them, learning Spanish or any other second language is relatively easy, because their brains are learning naturally. It's part of human development. Then we reach puberty and everything changes! Your body sets its speech pattern for your native language. This age is the time when the body's language learning center slows down or turns completely off for many people. Your body just figures it doesn't need it anymore. Coincidentally, this slow-down occurs about the time that you hit your seventh grade Spanish class. That's why learning Spanish seemed to be so hard—that, and the huge amount of very impractical things you were forced to learn. As a result of this physical change in puberty, adults tend to learn languages more visually. Listening and imitating are still important; especially when paired with a visual cue. Most adults benefit from seeing a Spanish word spelled phonetically and hearing it at the same time. This combination helps your brain make sense of the new sounds.

Adults are also practical learners. If you see a reason for what you are learning, you will find it easier to accomplish. It is very true that if you practice your Spanish daily, you are less likely to lose it.

If you did take Spanish in high school or college, you are going to be pleasantly surprised when words and phrases you thought you had forgotten begin to come back to you. That previous experience with other languages is still in your mind. It's just hidden away in a little-used filing cabinet. Soon that cabinet will open up again and that's going to help you learn new words even faster.

Here's another thought you should consider. *What they told you in the traditional foreign language classroom was not exactly correct.* There's no such thing as *"perfect Spanish"* just as there is no *"perfect English."* This fact leaves the door for good communication wide open!

The secret to learning Spanish is having *self-confidence and a great sense of humor*. To build self-confidence, you must realize that the entire learning experience is painless and fun. Naturally, you are going to make mistakes. Everyone does. We all make mistakes in English too! So get ready to laugh and learn. *Don't think that you have to have a perfect Spanish sentence in your head before you say something.* It's very important for you to say what you know —even if it's only a word or two. The point is to communicate. Communication doesn't have to be "pretty" or perfect to be effective.

Español is one of the world's most precise and expressive languages. Consider these other important facts as you begin to "*habla español*":

- ✓ English and Spanish share a common Latin heritage, so literally thousands of words in our two languages are either *similar* or *identical.*

- ✓ Your ability to communicate is the most important thing, so your grammar and pronunciation don't have to be "*perfect*" for you to be understood.

- ✓ Some very practical and common expressions in Spanish can be communicated with a few simple words.

- ✓ As the number of Latinos in the United States increases, so do your opportunities to practice. Saying even a phrase or two in Spanish every day will help you learn faster.

- ✓ Relax! People who enjoy their learning experiences acquire Spanish at a much faster pace than others.

- ✓ Set realistic goals and establish reasonable practice habits.

- ✓ When you speak even a little Spanish, you are showing a tremendous respect for the Hispanic culture and its people.

- ✓ Even a little Spanish or *poco español* goes a long way!

As you begin the process of learning Spanish, you are going to notice a few important differences. Speaking Spanish is going to feel and sound a little odd to you at first. This feeling is completely normal because you are using muscles in your face that English doesn't require, and your inner ear is not accustomed to hearing you speak Spanish. People tell me it sounds and feels like a cartoon character has gotten inside your head! Don't let that stop you. Just keep right on going!

Many Americans know more Spanish than they realize and they can pronounce many words perfectly. Review the list below. How many of the Spanish words in it, do you recognize? Using what you already know about Spanish will enable you to learn new things easier and faster—it's a great way to build your confidence.

Amigos Similares y Familiares

Americano	Amigo	Hospital	Español	Doctor
Loco	Hotel	Oficina	Agua	Fiesta
Dinero	Señor	Señorita	Señora	Sombrero
Burrito	Taco	Olé	No problema	Accidente
Nachos	Salsa	Teléfono	Quesadilla	Margarita
Tequila	Tortilla	Bueno	Grande	Mucho
Blanco	Adiós	Gracias	Feliz Navidad	Hasta la vista
Por favor	Pronto	Sí	Aplicación	Cinco de mayo

The Sounds of Spanish

No se preocupe. Don't worry. One of your biggest concerns about acquiring a new language will be speaking it well enough so that others can understand you. In many ways Spanish is close enough to English that making a few mistakes along the way won't hurt your ability to communicate.

The most important sounds in Spanish consist of *five* vowels. Each one is pronounced the way it is written. Spanish vowels are never *silent*. Even if there are two vowels together in a word, both of them will stand up and be heard.

A (ah) as in mama
E (eh) as in "hay or the "eh" in set
I (ee) as in deep
O (oh) as in open
U (oo) as in spoon

Here are the other sounds you'll need to remember. Always pronounce them the same way. Spanish is a very consistent language. The sounds the letters make don't shift around as much as they do in English.

Spanish Letter		English Sound
C	(before an e or i)	s as in Sam: **cero**: SAY-row
G	(before an e or i)	h as in he: **energía**: n-air-HE-ah
		emergencia: a-mare-HEN-see-ah
H		silent: **hacienda**: ah-see-N-da
J		h as in hot: **Julio**, HOO-lee-oh
LL		y as in yoyo: **tortilla**, tor-TEE-ya
Ñ		ny as in canyon: **español**, es-pan-NYOL
QU		k as in kit: **tequila**, tay-KEY-la
RR		"trilled" r sound: **burro**, BOO-row
V		v as in Victor: **Victor**, Vic-TOR
Z		s as in son: **Gonzales**, gone-SA-les

The Other Consonants: The remaining letters in Spanish have very similar sounds to their equivalents in English.

Note: People from Latin American countries have a variety of accents just like Americans do. A variety of accents is common in languages that are spoken over a wide geographic area. In certain areas of Latin America people tend to pronounce the letter "v" more like the English letter "b." This accent is particularly true in some parts of Mexico. In other Latin American countries a "v" sounds like an English "v." If you learned to switch the "v" sound for a "b" sound in high school or college Spanish classes, don't change your habit; however, if you haven't had any experience with Spanish before now, don't sweat the small stuff! Pronounce the "v" as you normally would.

The Spanish Alphabet
El alfabeto español

A	ah	J	HO-ta	R	AIR-ray
B	bay	K	ka	RR	EH-rray
C	say	L	L-ay	S	S-ay
CH	chay	LL	A-yea	T	tay
D	day	M	M-ay	U	oo
E	A or EH	N	N-ay	V	vay
F	f-ay	Ñ	N-yea	W	DOE-blay-vay
G	hay	O	oh	X	A-kees
H	AH-chay	P	pay	Y	ee-gree-A-gah
I	ee	Q	coo	Z	SAY-ta

Did you notice something different about the Spanish alphabet? It has four letters the English alphabet doesn't have. Can you find them?

The Four "Extra" Letters

Look carefully at the table above which contains the Spanish alphabet. Did you notice that the Spanish language has more letters in its alphabet than English does? There are thirty letters in the Spanish alphabet. Even though Spanish has more letters in its alphabet, none of them will present *problemas* for you. Here are the four extra letters and words in which they are used:

CH   Sounds like the following English words: Chuck, Charlie, and Chocolate. Try saying these Spanish words: nacho and macho.

LL Sounds essentially like an English "y." However, you will hear slight variations depending on where the person is from who is speaking Spanish to you. Example: Tortilla (tor-**T**-ya)

Ñ Sounds like a combination of "ny" as in canyon or onion. Example: español (es-pan-**NYOL**).

RR This letter is a "trilled" sound. Practice by taking your tongue and placing it in the roof of your mouth just behind your front teeth. Now blow air across the tip of your tongue and make it flutter. This sound can be difficult for some adults to make. It's only strange because you are moving your tongue muscle in a new way. Since there are no words in English with trilled sounds, you just never learned to move your tongue that way. Children learning Spanish have no trouble with this sound at all. Like any new activity, it will take time, patience and practice! Don't let a problem with the trilled "r" stop you from speaking. Essentially the sounds of the English "r" and the Spanish "r" are the same. To start with, say the double "r" a bit louder than a single "r."**Example:** Burrito (boo-**REE**-toe)

The Spanish Accent

In Spanish you will see two types of accent marks. Both marks are very important and do different things. One of the marks you will notice is called a "tilde." It is only found over the letter "N." But, don't get the Ñ confused with N. The accent mark over Ñ makes it into a different letter entirely. In fact, it's one of four letters in the Spanish alphabet that the English alphabet doesn't have. The Ñ changes the sound of the letter to a combination of "ny." You'll hear the sound that this important letter makes in the English words "canyon" and "onion."

Occasionally you will see another accent mark over a letter in a Spanish word. The accent mark or "slash" mark shows you where to place vocal emphasis. So, when you see an accent mark over a letter in a Spanish word, just say that part of the word louder. For example: José (ho-**SAY**). These accented syllables are indicated in your pronunciation guides with bold, capital letters.

Pronouncing Spanish Words

The pronunciation of Spanish words follows very basic, consistent rules. This regular pattern makes it easier to learn. Here are some tips to remember:

1. Most Spanish words that end with vowels are stressed or emphasized on the *next to the last* syllable.

    Señorita: sen-your-**REE**-ta   Jalapeño: ha-la-**PAIN**-yo

2. Look for an accent mark. If the Spanish word has an accent in it, that's the emphasized syllable.

    José: ho-**SAY**   ¿Cómo está?: **CO**-mo es-**TA**

3. Words that end in consonants are stressed on the *final* syllable.

    Doctor: doc-**TOR**   Hotel: oh-**TELL**

Spanish Punctuation Marks

Spanish has two different punctuation marks than English does. Both of them are upside down versions of English punctuation marks. They are used to signal that something besides a simple declarative sentence is ahead.

First, there's the upside down question mark (¿). You will see it at the beginning of all questions. It's there to let you know that what follows is a question and you will need to give your voice an upward inflection. It's the same sort of inflection we use in English.

Example: Do you speak English?   ¿Habla inglés?

Next, there's the upside down exclamation mark (¡). It's there to let you know that what follows should be vocally emphasized.

Example: Hi!   ¡Hola!

Spanglish

Much of the southwestern part of the United States originally belonged to Mexico. In 1848, after the US-Mexican War, the border was moved south to the Rio Grande River. The treaty that was signed at the end of the conflict transformed Spanish-speaking Mexicans into Americans overnight! Imagine waking up one morning and finding out that you are a citizen of another country — and that you have to learn a new language! As a result, an entirely new slang language was born that mixes the best of both worlds: *Spanglish*.

In America, Spanglish really started to come into its own in the early 1970s. At that time it gained both in popularity and vocabulary. Now, people who use Spanglish span generations, classes, and nationalities. It's heard in pop music, seen in print, and used in conversations throughout Latin America. It isn't just an American phenomenon. Immigrants may turn to Spanglish out of necessity while they are learning English, and bilingual speakers use it because it's convenient. If you listen to native speakers carefully, you will hear them use a mixture of languages. Sometimes in the middle of a conversation, you may hear an English word or two. People who speak Spanish tend to use whatever word or phrase suits their purpose and is most descriptive. In general conversation it doesn't matter what language it is. Even though Spanglish is still frowned upon in most traditional language classes and by those who want to keep the Spanish language "pure," it really is a great tool for most people.

Common Spanglish Words

Truck/Trocka	Lunch/Lonche	No parking/No parque
Yard/Yarda	Break/Breaka	Cell phone/Cel
Carpet/Carpeta	Check/Chequear	Market/Marketa
Push/Puchar	Roof/Ruffo	Email/Email

More Amigos Familiares

Using what you've learned about Spanish sounds, practice the words listed below. Examine them carefully. Each word bears a strong resemblance to its English counterpart or it is a common Spanish word. Begin by slowly pronouncing each word on the list. If you are having trouble, go back and review the vowel sounds. Continue by reviewing the section on Spanish accents and pronunciation. Reviewing these concepts will help you as you continue building your skills.

Accidente	Dieta	Margarina
Agua	Espagueti	Melón
Alcohol	Espátula	Mermelada
Autoservicio	Esponja	Orden
Banquete	Estómago	Panqueques
Bebé	Familia	Pera
Brócoli	Filtro	Picante
Cacerola	Flan	Piña
Café	Fruta	Plato
Café descafeinado	Hotel	Refrigerador
Caliente	Identificación	Restaurante
Cantalupo	Importante	Rosbif
Carne	Inglés	Sándwich
Carro	Inspección	Servicio
Chorizo	Jamón	Té
Cliente	Leche	Teléfono
Colador	Limón	Tomate
Coliflor	Macarrones	Tortilla
Crema	Maíz	Uniforme
Espárrago	Máquina	Vino

Muchos Ways to "Practicar"

The more you listen to and use your *español,* the easier it will be to learn it. There are lots of ways to practice, that won't cost you any money. Try these super techniques for improving your skills:

- ✓ Next time you're at a Mexican restaurant, order your food in *español*.
- ✓ Start slowly. Practice one sound each week.
- ✓ Read Spanish language newspapers. They are usually free and easily available.
- ✓ Listen to Spanish language radio stations.
- ✓ Watch Spanish language television.
- ✓ Rent Spanish language videos; especially cartoons.

- ✓ Buy Spanish tapes and listen to them in the car while you commute.
- ✓ And — speaking of tapes, there is such a variety of Latin *música* available, something will be right for you. Listening to music is a great way to train your ears to Spanish and have fun doing it. Personally, I like anything by Carlos Santana or the Salsa of Marc Anthony. What do you like?
- ✓ Visit Internet sites like *www.about.com* or *www.studyspanish.com*. You can find all kinds of information there about the Spanish language. They have a wonderful, free newsletter that comes to you via e-mail. Most search engines have some sort of Spanish section. An on-line search will turn up lots of treasures!
- ✓ Next time you listen to a baseball game, keep track of all the Hispanic names you hear.
- ✓ Speak Spanish every time the opportunity presents itself. Practice is the only way to get over your nervousness.
- ✓ Try to learn with a friend at work and practice together.

**What practice habits work for you? Share them with us at:
info@speakeasyspanish.com**

SpeakEasy's Tips and Techniques for Comunicación

It's important to remember, when you're trying to communicate with a person who is "limited in English proficiency," *patience is a virtue*! Put yourself in their shoes and think how you would feel if the roles were reversed. Here are some easy things you can do to make the conversation easier for both of you.

- ✓ Speak slowly and distinctly.
- ✓ Do not use slang expressions.
- ✓ Get straight to the point! Unnecessary words cloud your meaning.
- ✓ Speak in a normal tone. Speaking *loudly* doesn't help anyone understand you any better!
- ✓ Look for cues to meaning in body language and facial expressions. Use gestures of your own to get your point across.
- ✓ You may not receive good eye contact. Do not interpret the lack of eye contact negatively.
- ✓ Latinos tend to stand closer to each other than North Americans do when they talk with each other, so your personal space could feel crowded. Stand your ground!
- ✓ Feel free to use gestures and body language of your own to communicate.
- ✓ Because of the way languages are learned, it is likely that the person you are talking to understands more of what you are saying, than he is able to verbalize. *So, be careful what you say!* No matter what the language, we always understand the bad words first!

Tips & Tidbits
Throughout your book look for the light bulb you see above. This section will give you helpful hints and cultural information designed to help you learn Spanish more easily.

Beginning Words And Phrases

Your Latino employees and customers will be delighted you are learning to speak *español*. Words like please and thank you show respect and courtesy that will go a long way towards helping you to establish good rapport.

English	Español	Guide
Hi!	¡Hola!	**OH**-la
How are you?	¿Cómo está?	**CO**-mo es-**TA**
Fine	Muy bien.	mooy b-**N**
So so	Así así	ah-**SEE** ah-**SEE**
Bad	Mal	mal
Good morning	Buenos días	boo-**WAY**-nos **D**-ahs
Good afternoon	Buenas tardes	boo-**WAY**-nas **TAR**-days
Good night	Buenas noches.	boo-**WAY**-nas **NO**-chase
Sir or Mister	Señor	sen-**YOUR**
Mrs. or Ma'am	Señora	sen-**YOUR**-ah
Miss	Señorita	sen-your- **REE**-ta
What's your name?	¿Cómo se llama?	**CO**-mo say **YA**-ma
My name is ___	Me llamo ___.	may **YA**-mo
Nice to meet you	Mucho gusto	**MOO**-cho **GOO**-stow
Thank you.	Gracias.	**GRA**-see-ahs
Please	Por favor	pour-fa-**VOR**
You're welcome.	De nada.	day **NA** da
The pleasure is mine.	El gusto es mío.	el **GOO**-stow es **ME**-oh
I'm sorry.	Lo siento.	low-see-**N**-toe
Excuse me.	¡Perdón!	pear-**DON**
See you later	¡Hasta lluego!	**AH**-sta la lou-**A**-go
Good-bye	Adiós	ah-dee-**OS**

Spanish Sounds Rápido — What Do I Do Now?

Be honest! One of the reasons you are hesitant to speak Spanish is that it sounds so fast! Naturally, you're afraid you won't understand. Here are some phrases that will help you. Make learning them a priority.

English	Español	Guide
I don't understand.	No comprendo.	no com-PREN-doe
Do you understand?	¿Comprende?	com-PREN-day
I speak a little Spanish.	Hablo poco español.	AH-blow POE-co es-pan-NYOL
Do you speak English?	¿Habla inglés?	AH-bla eng-LACE
Repeat, please.	Repita, por favor.	ray-PETE-ah pour fa-VOR
I'm studying Spanish.	Estudio español.	es-TOO-d-oh es-pan-NYOL
Write it, please	Escribe, por favor.	es-SCREE-bay pour fa-VOR
Speak more slowly, please.	Habla más despacio, por favor.	AH-bla mas des-PA-see-oh pour fa-VOR
Thanks for your patience.	Gracias por su paciencia.	GRA-see-ahs pour sue pa-see-N-see-ah
How do you say it in Spanish?	¿Cómo se dice en español?	CO-mo say DEE-say n es-pan-NYOL
Where are you from?	¿De dónde es?	day DON-day es
May I help you?	¿Puedo servirle?	pooh-A-doe ser-VEER-lay

**Note: Verbs in this section are present tense.

The key here is not to pánico. Your Spanish-speaking employee or customer is having just as much trouble understanding you, as you are having understanding them! Hang in there! Between the two of you, *comunicación* will begin to take place.

Conversations to Practice

Practice Conversation I

USTED (YOU):	Good morning, Sir.
SR. GARCÍA	Good morning. How are you?
USTED	Fine, thanks. How are you?
SR. GARCÍA	OK, thanks.

Practice Conversation II

USTED: May I help you? My name is _____. I speak a little Spanish. What's your name?

SRA. GARCÍA: My name is Carla García-Hernandez. I speak a little English.

USTED: Nice to meet you.

SRA. GARCÍA: Yes, nice to meet you.

Using phrases found on pages 14-15, practice the following.

- ✓ A greeting of your choice.
- ✓ My name is _____.
- ✓ I speak a little Spanish.
- ✓ Do you speak English?
- ✓ Speak more slowly, please.
- ✓ Thank you.

¿Cuál Es Su Nombre Completo?
What Is Your <u>Complete</u> Name?

Hispanic Names Have Four Parts

First Name Primer Nombre	Middle Name Segundo Nombre	Father's Surname Apellido Paterno	Mother's Surname Apellido Materno
Carlos	Jesús	Santana	Rodríguez
Poncho	Luis	Villa	García
Carmen	Elena	Miranda	Rivera

Start with: Señor, Señora,   or   Señorita

Use Both Names Or Only The Father's Last Name

Sr. Santana   Sr. Villa   Sra. Miranda

When a Woman Marries

She <u>keeps</u> her father's Apellido Paterno, and she <u>drops</u> her Apellido Materno
In place of her Apellido Materno is her husband's Apellido Paterno

Children Have The Apellido Paterno of
Both Father and Mother

If Carlos Santana married Carmen Miranda Rivera,
what would her name be after the marriage? What's the complete name
of their child?

José Carlos ???? ?????

Answer: 1. Carmen Miranda-Santana   2. José Carlos Santana Miranda

Spanish Nouns
Can words *really* have a gender?

¡Sí! Spanish belongs to the "romance" language family. It doesn't have anything to do with love, but it has a lot to do with the Romans. In ancient times, people had the same trouble learning languages that they do today—except that there were no cassette tapes, CDs, PDAs or very many foreign language teachers. In those days, there weren't many schools for that matter! Consequently, most people were on their own when it came to learning another language.

To help the difficult process along, words were placed into categories based upon how they sounded. It organized the material and made it easier to learn. Old world languages had categories that were often described as "masculine," "feminine," or even "neuter." From these descriptions, people began talking about words in terms of their gender. Even though the word "gender" is misleading, the tendency to group words by sound helped people learn new languages more quickly.

Because Spanish evolved from Latin, it has maintained two category divisions for thousands of years. The categories are called masculine and feminine. Even though Spanish can and will evolve, the concept of categories in *español* is not likely to change.

Here are the most important points to remember about nouns and their categories:

1. Usually, the words are grouped by how they sound, not by what they mean. There will always be a few exceptions!

2. Languages are a lot like the people who use them: They don't always follow the rules!

3. If the Spanish noun is referring to a person, the letter will often indicate the sex of that individual. For example: a doctor, who is a man, is a "*doctor*," while a woman, who is a doctor, is a "*doctora*."

4. Words in the "masculine" category usually end with the letter "O".

NOUN A person, place or thing

5. Words in the "feminine" category usually end with the letter "A".
6. El, la, los and las are very important words. They all mean "the". They are the clues you need to tell you a word's category.

El (masculine category – singular)	El niño, El muchacho
Los (masculine category – plural)	Los niños, Los muchachos
La (feminine category – singular)	La niña, La muchacha
Las (feminine category – plural)	Las niñas, Las muchachas

ADJECTIVE: Describes a noun

A Word about Adjectives

Describing things in Spanish can present problems for English speakers. There are several reasons why using adjectives may give us trouble. First, there is the position of the adjective in relation to the noun. In English, descriptive words go in front of the noun like "white cat," for example. In Spanish, the noun is the most important element, so it comes first. White cat is *un gato blanco*. It is the opposite of our word order. However, it gets more complicated because there are a few basic adjectives which show size or quantity that are placed in front of the noun, just like English. These include words like large (*grande*) and small (*pequeño*), along with numbers. For example: a large white cat is *un grande gato blanco*.

Second, since Spanish nouns are divided into masculine and feminine categories, the adjective must match its noun by category. This means that from time to time you will need to match the letter at the end of the adjective and make it the same letter that is at the end of the noun. You must also match the adjective to the noun by number (singular or plural). This matching sound feature of Spanish is one of the main reasons it has such a musical sound.

Here is an example:
One large white house = *Una grande casa blanca*
Six large white houses = *Seis grandes casas blancas*

Common Adjectives — Adjetivos Comunes

These common adjectives are shown as you would find them in a Spanish dictionary. As written, use them with singular words in the masculine category, and place them behind the noun. Change the "o" at the end to an "a" to make them match up with words in the feminine category. Don't forget to add an "s" at the end for plural words.

English	Español	English	Español
Good	Bueno	Bad	Malo
Better	Mejor	Worse	Peor
Big	Grande	Small	Pequeño
Clean	Limpio	Dirty	Sucio
Hot	Caliente	Cold	Frío
Safe	Seguro	Dangerous	Peligroso
Easy	Fácil	Difficult	Difícil
Full	Lleno	Empty	Vacío
Fast	Rápido	Slow	Lento
New	Nuevo	Old	Viejo
Pretty	Bonito	Ugly	Feo
Quiet	Tranquilo	Restless	Inquieto
Tall	Alto	Short	Bajo
Well	Bien	Sick	Enfermo
Strong	Fuerte	Weak	Débil

Tips & Tidbits

Remember that learning the noun is the most important thing, not which category or gender it is! Words like "el" or "la" only mean "the." They don't give any clues to what you are trying to say. Learning the fine points of grammar can wait until you become a master of communications using Survival Spanish.

The Essentials of Spanish Verbs

There are basically three types of regular verbs in Spanish. The last two letters on the end of the verb determines how it is to be treated. Listed below are the three most common types of regular verb endings.

- ✓ **AR** – Hablar: To speak
- ✓ **ER** – Comprender: To understand
- ✓ **IR** – Escribir: To write

VERB: Shows action or state of being

In Survival Spanish, we focus on speaking about ourselves and talking to another person. That's the most common type of "one-on-one" communication.

When you need to say I speak, I understand, or I live, change the last two letters of the verb to an "O".

- ✓ Hablo
- ✓ Comprendo
- ✓ Escribo

When asking a question, such as do you speak, do you understand, or do you live, change the ending to an "a" or an "e". *The change in letter indicates that you are speaking to someone else.*

- ✓ Habla
- ✓ Comprende
- ✓ Escribe

To make a sentence negative, simply put "no" in front of the verb.

- ✓ No hablo
- ✓ No comprendo
- ✓ No escribo

¡Acción!

There are so many English friendly *acción* words in the Spanish "AR" verb family. Many of them bear a strong resemblance to English verbs—most of them share a simple, regular nature. They are a very important asset in on-the-job communication. We picked a few of our favorites to get you started. Look closely at the list on the next page. On it you will recognize many comforting similarities between our languages that are practical too! Changing one letter will really expand your conversational skills.

In on-the-job conversations, people tend to use "I" and "you" to start many sentences. Of all the pronouns, these two are the most powerful and will work the best for you. That's where we'll start.

Here's an important difference between our languages. In English, the use of pronouns is essential because most of our verbs tend to end the same way. For example, with I speak and you speak; the verb "speak" remains the same. In English, our pronouns make all the difference. Spanish is different in this aspect. Spanish-speaking people are listening for the letters on the end of the verb. That's what indicates who or what is being talked about in Spanish. Each ending is different. The end of the Spanish verb is much more important than the beginning. The ending of the verb tells the Spanish-speaking person who or what is being discussed. In most cases when people speak Spanish, you might not hear a pronoun. It's not necessary for precise meaning. That's a big reason why Spanish might sound a little fast to you:

Pronouns, which are important in English, are routinely eliminated in Spanish!

Try this: Treat the verbs in the "AR" family as you would "to speak" or "hablar." End the verb with an "o" when you're talking about yourself; "hablo" or "I speak". Change the verb ending from an "o" to an "a" for "habla" or "you speak." Use this form when you're talking to someone else.

English	Español	Guide
I need	Necesito	nay-say-SEE-toe
You need	Necesita	nay-say-SEE-ta

The Sweet Sixteen Verbs

This list contains sixteen of the most commonly used regular verbs in the "AR" verb family. Since they are so practical for use on the job, begin learning them and using them first.

English	Español	Guide
To need	Necesitar	nay-say-see-**TAR**
To use	Usar	oo-**SAR**
To prepare	Preparar	pray-pa-**RAR**
To cook	Cocinar	co-see-**NAR**
To work	Trabajar	tra-baa-**HAR**
To mix	Mezclar	mess-**CLAR**
To call	Llamar	ya-**MAR**
To clean	Limpiar	leem-p-**ARE**
To help	Ayudar	eye-you-**DAR**
To ask	Preguntar	prey-goon-**TAR**
To carry	Llevar	yea-**VAR**
To roast	Asar	ah-**CZAR**
To wash	Lavar	la-**VARE**
To sweep	Informar	een-for-**MAR**
To pay	Pagar	pa-**GAR**
To return	Regresar	ray-grey-**SAR**

**Note: To make a sentence negative, say no in front of the verb.
   Example: I don't need. **No necesito.** You don't need **No necesita.**

Which verbs in the Sweet 16 do you use most often? List your top five:

1. _____

2. _____

3. _____

4. _____

5. _____

> **Tú and Usted**
>
> In español there are two words for "you": Usted and tú.
>
> Usted is for adults, strangers, and acquaintances.
> Tú is for children and close friends.
>
> When using usted, your verb will end in the letter "a."
>
> When using tú, your verb should end with "as."

Now take your top five and change the AR ending to an "a" to indicate you are talking to someone else. Example: habla meaning you speak.

1. _____

2. _____

3. _____

4. _____

5. _____

¡Necesito una breaka! ¿Y usted?

Irregular Verbs: The Big Five

Now that you have had the opportunity to learn about the tremendous number of verbs that follow regular patterns in Spanish, it's time to take a look at others that don't follow the rules. They are unpredictable, but they are very important. In fact, they reflect some of man's oldest concepts. That's why they tend to be irregular. These words were in use long before language rules and patterns were set. There are two verbs in Spanish that mean "to be." The others are: to have, to make and to go. Because they don't follow the rules, you will need to memorize them, but that should be easy because you will use and hear them often.

In English, the "to be" verb is I am, you are, he is, etc. The Spanish version is **ser** and **estar**. *Ser* is used to express permanent things like your nationality or profession. *Estar* is used when talking about location or conditions that change like a person's health.

SER
Yo **soy**	Nosotros **somos**
Tú **eres**	
Él **es**	Ellos **son**
Ella **es**	Ellas **son**
Usted **es**	Ustedes **son**

ESTAR
Yo **estoy**	Nosotros **estamos**
Tú **estás**	
Él **está**	Ellos **están**
Ella **está**	Ellas **están**
Usted **está**	Ustedes **están**

The verb *"to have"* in Spanish is *muy importante*. In English, we say that we are hot, cold, hungry, thirsty, right, wrong, or sleepy, but in Spanish those are conditions that you have. Some of those expressions mean something totally different than you expected if you get the verbs confused, so be careful!

TENER
Yo **tengo**	Nosotros **tenemos**
Tú **tienes**	
Él **tiene**	Ellos **tienen**
Ella **tiene**	Ellas **tienen**
Usted **tiene**	Ustedes **tienen**

In Spanish, the verb that means, *"to do"* also means, *"to make."* It's not unusual for one verb to have multiple meanings. There are many expressions that require the use of this verb, but you will use it most when you talk about the weather. That's a safe subject and one that everyone, the world over, discusses! **¿Qué tiempo hace?** What's the weather? **Hace frío.** (It's cold.) **Hace sol.** (It's sunny). **Hace calor.** (It's hot) **Hace viento** (It's windy.). Here are two exceptions: **Está lloviendo** (It's raining.) and **Está nevando.** (It's snowing.)

HACER

Yo **hago**	Nosotros **hacemos**
Tú **haces**	
Él **hace**	Ellos **hacen**
Ella **hace**	Ellas **hacen**
Usted **hace**	Ustedes **hacen**

The last of the big five is perhaps the easiest to use. It's the verb that means, *"to go"*. In Spanish, that's *ir*. It's pronounced like the English word ear. Both in English and in Spanish, we use parts of it to make the future tense, in other words, to talk about things that we are going to do. Look at the parts of *ir*. Then look back at the parts of the verb *ser*. Do you see any similarities?

IR

Yo **voy**	Nosotros **vamos**
Tú **vas**	
Él **va**	Ellos **van**
Ella **va**	Ellas **van**
Usted **va**	Ustedes **van**

When you want to say something that you are going to do, start with I'm going or *voy*. Next, insert the word *"a"* and the basic verb that states what it is that you're going to do. Try it! It's easy. Here are some examples.

Voy a visitar a mi familia.	I am going to visit my family.
Voy a organizar el proyecto.	I am going to organize the project.
Mario va a comprar las plantas.	Mario is going to buy the plants.

**Note: The whole concept of irregular verbs can be quite daunting. Don't let it defeat you! We have many irregular verbs in English. Every language has them. The only way to master them is to use them. Make them your own! Try writing different parts of a verb on your desk calendar. That way, it will be there in front of you every time you look down. When you see it, say it to yourself. Then, you'll have it conquered in no time.

Are You Hungry? — ¿Tiene Hambre?

Using the right verb at the right time is very important. The following common expressions in Spanish require the use of *tener*. These are phrases you must learn, even though the translation will feel strange to you. *Remember our English idioms often sound very strange to non-native speakers.*

As a rule, *tener* is used to describe physical conditions. In English we use the verb *to be* instead.

TENER: *To have*   **TENGO**: *I have*   **TIENE**: *You have*

English	Español	Guide
Hot	Calor	ca-**LORE**
Hungry	Hambre	**AM**-bray
Cold	Frío.	**FREE**-oh
Ashamed	Vergüenza	ver-goo-**N**-sa
In pain.	Dolor	doe-**LORE**
Afraid of	Miedo de	me-**A**-doe day
Right	Razón	rah-**SEWN**
Thirsty	Sed	said
Sleepy	Sueño	soo-**WAYNE**-nyo
xx years old	*xx* años	*xx* **AHN**-nyos

What's The Weather? — ¿Qué Tiempo Hace?

No matter what the culture is a general topic for discussion is always the weather. Discussing the weather in Spanish requires a different verb from the one used in English. If you say to your host, "*Está frío*," he or she would think that you were talking about something you had touched. In Spanish, use the verb **hacer** which means to do or to make to describe the weather. It's one of the big five irregulars.

English	Español	Guide
What's the weather?	¿Qué tiempo hace?	kay t-M-po AH-say
To be nice weather	Hace buen tiempo	AH-say boo-WAYNE t-M-po
To be hot	Hace calor	AH-say ca-LORE
To be cool	Hace fresco	AH-say FRES-co
To be sunny	Hace sol	AH-say sol
To be windy	Hace viento	AH-say v-N-toe
To be cold	Hace frío	AH-say FREE-oh
Rain	Lluvia	U-v-ah
To rain.	Llover	YO-ver

Tips & Tidbits

In America we use the Fahrenheit scale for measuring the temperature. Latin Americans countries use the Celsius scale. Do you know what the difference is? Here's a simple example: 0 degrees Celsius is 32 degrees Fahrenheit.

Special Uses of Ser and Estar

The verbs *ser* and *estar* both mean the same thing in English: *to be,* but *how can two verbs mean the same thing?* It's because *ser* and *estar* are used in very different ways. Spanish sees these two verbs differently and uses them in very precise ways. Listed below are some simple guidelines on their usage:

Common Uses of Ser

A. **To express an permanent quality or characteristic**

El plato es de porcelana.	The plate is made of porcelain.
El restaurante es enorme.	The restaurant is enormous.
Los cocineros son importantes.	Cooks are important.

B. **To describe or identify**

Mi amigo es un chef.	My friend is a chef.
El mesero es alto.	The waiter is tall.

C. **To indicate nationality**

Pedro es mexicano.	Pedro is Mexican.
La salsa es de Argentina.	The sauce is from Argentina.

D. **To express ownership**

Este es mi auto.	This is my car.
Este es mi libro.	This is my book.

E. **To express time and dates**

¿Qué hora es?	What time is it?
Hoy es el nueve de junio.	Today is the 9th of June.

F.   With impersonal expressions.

Es importante estudiar.	It's important to study.
Es necesario leer.	It's necessary to read.

Common Uses of Estar

A.   To express location

Estoy en la cocina.	I am in the kitchen.
Charlotte está en Carolina del Norte.	Charlotte is in North Carolina.
El baño está en el segundo piso.	The bathroom is on the 2nd floor.

B.   To indicate someone's health

Mi esposa está enferma.	My wife is sick.
¿Cómo está usted?	How are you?

C.   Estar is also used as a helping verb

Estoy hablando.	I am speaking.
Carmen está trabajando.	Carmen is working.
Julio está regresando mañana.	Julio is returning tomorrow.

Tips & Tidbits

Notice from the examples that *ser* is used more frequently than *estar*. Even though the usage of *ser* and *estar* seems complicated in the beginning, both verbs are used so frequently in conversation that you will become comfortable using them quickly. Begin with the "I" or "yo" form of each verb. Next, tackle the "you" or "usted" form. You will use those two forms of the verb's conjugation much more than the other parts of it.

The Numbers — Los Números

When you are talking to a native speaker and you are discussing anything involving numbers, keep the following important information in mind:

1. Most people say numbers **extremely** fast! Don't hesitate to ask for a number to be said more slowly or to be repeated. Review the chapter called **Spanish Sounds Rápido — What Do I Do Now?**

2. When native speakers are saying phone numbers, many pair the numbers together instead of saying them as single digits.

3. If you are expressing a date which contains the year, often a native speaker will say the complete number. For example: 1962 will be said "one thousand nine hundred sixty and two" or "**mil novecientos sesenta y dos.**" If you wish, it is also correct to pair the numbers as "nineteen sixty-two" or "diez y nueve sesenta y dos."

Number	Español	Guide
0	Cero	**SAY**-row
1	Uno	**OO**-no
2	Dos	dose
3	Tres	trays
4	Cuatro	coo-**AH**-trow
5	Cinco	**SINK**-oh
6	Seis	**SAY**-ees
7	Siete	see-**A**-tay
8	Ocho	**OH**-cho
9	Nueve	new-**A**-vay

Number	Español	Guide
10	Diez	d-ACE
11	Once	ON-say
12	Doce	DOSE-a
13	Trece	TRAY-say
14	Catorce	ca-TOR-say
15	Quince	KEEN-say
16	Diez y seis	d-ACE e SAY-ees
17	Diez y siete	d-ACE e see-ATE-tay
18	Diez y ocho	d-ACE e OH-cho
19	Diez y nueve	d-ACE e new-A-vay
20	Veinte	VAIN-tay
21	Veinte y uno	VAIN-tay e OO-no
22	Veinte y dos	VAIN-tay e dose
23	Veinte y tres	VAIN-tay e trays
24	Veinte y cuatro	VAIN-tay e coo-AH-trow
25	Veinte y cinco	VAIN-tay e SINK-oh
26	Veinte y seis	VAIN-tay e SAY-ees
27	Veinte y siete	VAIN-tay e see-A-tay
28	Veinte y ocho	VAIN-tay e OH-cho -
29	Veinte y nueve	VAIN-tay e new-A-vay
30	Treinta	TRAIN-ta

Number	Español	Guide
40	Cuarenta	kwah-**RAIN**-ta
50	Cincuenta	seen-**KWAIN**-ta
60	Sesenta	say-**SAIN**-ta
70	Setenta	say-**TAIN**-ta
80	Ochenta	oh-**CHAIN**-ta
90	Noventa	no-**VAIN**-ta
100	Cien	see-**IN**
200	Doscientos	dose-see-**N**-tos
300	Trescientos	tray-see-**N**-tos
400	Cuatrocientos	coo-**AH**-troh-see-**N**-tos
500	Quinientos	keen-e-**N**-tos
600	Seiscientos	**SAY**-ees-see-**N**-tos
700	Setecientos	**SAY**-tay-see-**N**-tos
800	Ochocientos	**OH**-choh-see-**N**-tos
900	Novecientos	**NO**-vay-see-**N**-tos
1,000	Mil	meal

Para Practicar

1. Practice your home, office and cell phone number.
2. Practice saying the number for the date each day.
3. Practice saying the numbers on the license plates of cars in front of you when you are stopped in traffic.
4. Practice saying the numbers for highways near your home or office.

The Days of the Week and Months of the Year

Los Días de la Semana

English	Español	Guide
Monday	lunes	LOON-ace
Tuesday	martes	MAR-tays
Wednesday	miércoles	me-AIR-co-lace
Thursday	jueves	who-WAVE-ace
Friday	viernes	v-AIR-nace
Saturday	sábado	SAH-ba-doe
Sunday	domingo	doe-MING-go

When expressing a date in Spanish, give the number of the day first. Follow the day with the month. Use this format: El (date) de (month).

Los Meses del Año

English	Español	Guide
January	enero	n-NAY-row
February	febrero	fay-BRAY-row
March	marzo	MAR-so
April	abril	ah-BRILL
May	mayo	MY-oh
June	junio	WHO-knee-oh
July	julio	WHO-lee-oh
August	agosto	ah-GOS-toe
September	septiembre	sep-tee-EM-bray
October	octubre	oc-TOO-bray
November	noviembre	no-v-EM-bray
December	diciembre	d-see-EM-bray

Your appointment is (day of the week) el (number) de (month).
Su cita es lunes, el 11 de octubre.

Practicing Numbers & Dates

Practice these important items by using numbers, days of the week, and months of the year:

✓   Your social security number

✓   Your driver's license number

✓   The numbers in your address

✓   Your zip code

✓   Your phone number

✓   Your birth date

✓   Your children's birth dates

✓   The dates of holidays

✓   License tags of the cars in front of you, when you are stopped in traffic.

Combine the Spanish alphabet with this exercise.

✓   Phone numbers you see on billboards

✓   Numbers found on street signs

✓   Phone numbers when you dial them at work or at home

✓   The appointments on your personal calendar

✓   Your wedding anniversary

✓   The dates of all your Spanish classes or practice sessions

What Time Is It? — ¿Qué Hora Es?

The concept of time is something that varies from culture to culture. Many countries put less emphasis on being on time for certain things than Americans do. In Latino culture one lives for the present. It can be especially true in one's personal life; however, on the job everyone knows the value of *puntualidad*. *¡Es muy importante!*

Learning to tell time is another good way to put your numbers in Spanish to good use *¿Qué hora es?* means *what time is it?*

It's one o'clock.	Es la una.
It's two o'clock.	Son las dos.
It's 3:30.	Son las tres y media.
It's 5:45.	Son las seis menos quince.

Use the phrases *de la mañana* to indicate morning and *de la tarde* to indicate afternoon. Also midnight is *medianoche*. Noon is *mediodía*.

To find out at what time something takes place ask: *¿A qué hora…?*

¿A qué hora es la reunión?	What time is the meeting?
¿A qué hora termina?	What time do you finish?

Spanish speakers sometimes use the 24-hour clock for departures and arrivals of trains and flights, etc.

12:05	las doce cero cinco
17.52	las diez y siete cincuenta y dos
23.10	las veinte y tres diez
07.15	las siete quince

Para Practicar

Using the word for meeting "la reunion," say that your meeting takes place on the hour throughout your workday. La reunión es a las ocho.

Scheduling an Appointment

When you need to schedule an appointment or an interview with a perspective employee, this form will come in very handy for you. In *español* an appointment is called a *cita* (SEE-ta). List the name of the individual that the appointment is with first. Then circle the day of the week and add the number for the day. Finally, circle the month and add the time. The phrase at the bottom of this form simply asks the individual to arrive ten minutes early for the appointment.

Usted tiene una cita importante con _____.

La cita es	lunes	el _____ de	enero	a las _____.
	martes		febrero	
	miércoles		marzo	
	jueves		abril	
	viernes		mayo	
			junio	
			julio	
			agosto	
			septiembre	
			octubre	
			noviembre	
			diciembre	

**Favor de llegar 10 minutos antes del tiempo de su cita. ¡Gracias!
Please arrive 10 minutes before the time of your appointment. Thank you.

The Questions Everyone Should Know

English	Español	Guide
Who?	¿Quién?	key-N
What?	¿Qué?	kay
Which?	¿Cuál?	coo-ALL
When?	¿Cuándo?	KWAN-doe
Where?	¿Dónde?	DON-day
Why?	¿Por qué?	pour KAY
How?	¿Cómo?	CO-mo
What's happening?	¿Qué pasa?	kay PA-sa
How much?	¿Cuánto?	KWAN-toe
How many?	¿Cuántos?	KWAN-toes

When you ask a question in Spanish, it will take on the same form as a question does in English. Start with the question word that asks the information you need. Follow the question word with a verb, and give your voice an upward inflection.

In Spanish you can also make a question by ending your sentence with *¿no?* Here's an example: *Cancún está en México, ¿no?* When you end a sentence with "no" like this, it takes on the meaning of "isn't it."

The Most Common Questions

How are you?	¿Cómo está?
How much does it cost?	¿Cuánto cuesta?
Where are you from?	¿De dónde es?

To make the Spanish upside down question mark or the upside down exclamation mark refer, to the chapter called "Typing in Spanish on Your Computer."

Getting the Información

Listed below are common phrases that are used to fill out almost any questionnaire. It seems like most forms always ask for much of the same information in almost the same order. By learning a few simple phrases, you can use this format to your advantage.

There are so many times when we need to ask for very basic information. Most of these questions begin with the words "*what is your.*" When you are asking this type of question, remember that it's not always necessary to make a complete sentence to have good communication. The information you are asking for is much more important than the phrase "what is your"? As long as you remember to make what you say *sound* like a question by giving your voice an *upward* inflection, people will interpret what you've said *as* a question.

Use the form on the following page. It asks for very basic information. To help you practice, work with a partner. Make up new information about yourself and complete the form. At each practice session one of you will ask the questions and the other will give the answers to fill in the information requested. This is a great practice exercise, because when you think about it, most of the time the questions you ask will be the same, but the answers you get will always be different!

What's your. . .   ¿Cuál es su. . .
                              coo-ALL es sue

English	Español	Guide
Full name	Nombre completo	**NOM**-bray com-**PLAY**-toe
First name	Primer nombre	pre-**MARE** **NOM**-bray
Middle name	Segundo nombre	say-**GOON**-doe **NOM**-bray
Last name (surname)	Apellido	ah-pay-**YE**-doe
Paternal surname	Apellido paterno	ah-pay-**YE**-doe pa-**TER**-no

English	Español	Guide
Maternal surname	Apellido materno	ah-pay-YE-doe ma-TER-no
Address	Dirección	d-wreck-see-ON
Apartment number	Número de apartamento	NEW-may-row day ah-par-ta-MEN-toe
Age	Edad	a-DAD
Date of birth	Fecha de nacimiento	FAY-cha day na-see-me-N-toe
Nationality	Nacionalidad	na-see-on-nal-e-DAD
Place of birth	Lugar de nacimiento	loo-GAR day na-see-me-N-toe
Place of employment	Lugar de empleo	loo-GAR day m-PLAY-oh
Occupation	Ocupación	oh-coo-pa-see-ON
Home telephone number	Número de teléfono de su casa	NEW-may-row day tay-LAY-fo-no day sue CA-sa
Work telephone number	Número de teléfono de su empleo	NEW-may-row day tay-LAY-fo-no day sue m-PLAY-oh
Marital status	Estado civil	es-TA-doe see-VEAL
Married	Casado (a)	ca-SA-doe
Single	Soltero (a)	soul-TAY-row
Divorced	Divorciado (a)	d-vor-see-AH-doe
Widow	Viudo (a)	v-OO-doe
Separated	Separado (a)	sep-pa-RAH-doe
Driver's license number	Número de licencia	NEW-may-row day lee-SEN-see-ah
Social security number	Número de seguro social	NEW-may-row day say-GOO-row sew-see-AL

Información Básica
Imprima por favor

FECHA: _____
MES   DÍA   AÑO

SR.
SRA.
SRTA._____
  PRIMER NOMBRE   SEGUNDO NOMBRE   APELLIDO PATERNO   APELLIDO MATERNO (ESPOSO)

DIRECCIÓN: _____
                               CALLE

_____
CIUDAD   ESTADO   ZONA POSTAL

TELÉFONO: CASA _____   EMPLEO _____

           CEL _____   FAX _____

CORREO ELECTRÓNICO
_____

NÚMERO DE SEGURO SOCIAL: _____-_____-_____

FECHA DE NACIMIENTO   _____
                           MES   DÍA   AÑO

NÚMERO DE LA LICENCIA: _____

OCUPACIÓN: _____

LUGAR DE EMPLEO _____

ESTADO CIVIL: CASADO (A)   DIVORCIADO (A)
                  SOLTERO (A)   SEPARADO (A)
                  VIUDO (A)

NOMBRE DE ESPOSO: _____
       PRIMER NOMBRE   SEGUNDO NOMBRE   APELLIDO PATERNO   APELLIDO MATERNO/ESPOSO

NOMBRE DE ESPOSA: _____
       PRIMER NOMBRE   SEGUNDO NOMBRE   APELLIDO PATERNO   APELLIDO MATERNO/ESPOSO

EN CASO DE EMERGENCIA: _____   TELÉFONO: _____

FIRMA: _____   FECHA: _____

See back of book for English translation of the basic information form.

The Family — La Familia

Putting our families first is something all Americans have in common. It is especially true for Latinos. For them, family values are extremely important. No sacrifice is too great if it helps the family. Children are considered to be precious gifts. Wives, mothers, and grandmothers are highly respected. Remember that the maternal side of the family is so important that traditionally Hispanics carry their mother's surname or *materno apellido* as a part of their complete name. If you have forgotten the four important parts of a Latino's name, please review the chapter called *"Cuál es su nombre completo."*

You are certainly going to hear about members of the family from your Hispanic customers and employees. It's something all of us like to talk about!

English	Español	Guide
Aunt	Tía	T-ah
Uncle	Tío	T-oh
Brother	Hermano	air-**MAN**-oh
Sister	Hermana	air-**MAN**-ah
Brother-in-law	Cuñado	coon-**YA**-doe
Sister-in-law	Cuñada	coon-**YA**-da
Child	Niño *(m)*	**KNEE**-nyo
	Niña *(f)*	**KNEE**-nya
Cousin	Primo *(m)*	**PRE**-mo
	Prima *(f)*	**PRE**-ma
Daughter	Hija	E-ha
Son	Hijo	E-ho

English	Español	Guide
Daughter-in-law	Nuera	new-**AIR**-rah
Son-in-law	Yerno	**YAIR**-no
Father	Padre	**PA**-dray
Mother	Madre	**MA**-dray
Father-in-law	Suegro	soo-**A**-grow
Mother-in-law	Suegra	soo-**A**-gra
Niece	Sobrina	so-**BREE**-na
Nephew	Sobrino	so-**BREE**-no
Step father	Padrastro	pa-**DRAS**-tro
Step mother	Madrastra	ma-**DRAS**-tra
Step son	Hijastro	e-**HAS**-tro
Step daughter	Hijastra	e-**HAS**-tra
Granddaughter	Nieta	knee-**A**-ta
Grandson	Nieto	knee-**A**-toe
Grandfather	Abuelo	ah-boo-**A**-low
Grandmother	Abuela	ah-boo-**A**-la
Husband	Esposo	es-**POE**-so
Wife	Esposa	es-**POE**-sa

Para Practicar

Using the verb tener (to have), tell your practice partner how many relatives you have in your family. Start like this: Tengo or I have. Follow that with the number and the member of the family that you are talking about.

For example: Tengo una hermana. I have a sister.

Employee Benefits and Human Resources
Beneficios y Recoursos Humanos

As you might expect, employment practices are very different in Latin America than they are in the US. The concept of deductions for taxes and insurance might be completely new for a first generation Hispanic employee. It's very rare for a worker, especially an hourly wage earner, to receive benefits such as health insurance or paid vacations in Latin America. Your benefit package may be different in both concept and practice from what this employee has experienced before — explain it to him very slowly — especially if payroll deductions are involved. No one likes surprises on pay day.

For an important meeting like this one where you want to get started out on the right foot, it's important to be well-prepared. Make a check list of all the vocabulary you are likely to use. Practice pronouncing these words and phrases before the meeting takes place. Make as many notes as you want, and remember to go at your own speed. Take all the time you need! You will be able to communicate much more effectively if you aren't nervous. Your new employee will certainly appreciate your effort. Allow time and make the opportunity for your new hire to ask questions. The ability to express opinions and discuss options is highly valued in Latin American culture. Never close this important door to communications! This meeting marks the beginning of a valuable relationship you are building with this employee. After your conference is over, review your notes again. Mark the areas where you felt comfortable and did well. Highlight the areas where you feel you need more work or additional practice. Each time you need to explain benefits to a Spanish-speaking employee, you'll get better and better.

English	Español	Guide
Benefits	Beneficios	ben-nay-**FEE**-see-ohs
Check	Cheque	**CHEC**-kay
Disability	Incapacidad	n-ka-pah-see-**DAD**
Holidays	Días festivos	**DEE**-ahs fes-**T**-vos
Medical insurance	Seguro médico	say-**GOO**-row **MAY**-d-co
Overtime	Sobre tiempo	so-bray-t-**M**-po
Paid vacations	Vacaciones pagadas	va-ca-see-**ON**-ace pa-**GA**-das
Paycheck	Paga	**PAH**-ga
Permanent residence card	Tarjeta de residencia	tar-**HEY**-ta day ray-see-**DEN**-c-a
Retirement	Retiro Jubilación	ray-**TEE**-row who-bee-la-see-**ON**
Severance pay	Indemnización por despedida	in-dem-knee-za-see-**ON** pour days-pay-**DEE**-dah
Sick leave	Días pagados por enfermedad	**DEE**-ahs pah-**GA**-dos pour in-fer-may-**DAD**
Social security	Seguro social	say-**GOO**-row so-see-**AL**
Tax deductions	Deducciones de impuestos	day-dook-see-**ON**-aces day em-poo-**ES**-toes
Taxes	Impuestos	em-poo-**ES**-toes
Unemployment Insurance	Seguro de desempleo	say-**GOO**-row day des-em-**PLAY**-oh
Worker's Compensation	Compensación de obrero	com-pen-za-see-**ON** day o-**BRAY**-row

Motivation and Evaluation

Most companies require appraisals of their employee's performance at regular intervals. Job evaluations are very important for the business and the employee. Everyone appreciates knowing where they stand and getting some positive feedback! When evaluating a Latin American employee, keep these important tips in mind:

1. If your interview takes place in an office setting, make sure to get up from your desk. Then, walk around it to greet your employee and shake hands. Indicate where you wish them to sit.

2. If your office has a seating area away from your desk, take advantage of it. By sitting in a chair beside your employee, you will put him at ease. This removes the desk as an obstacle between you.

3. Don't "cut to the chase" and begin your evaluation immediately. Have some conversation first. Ask about your employee family. A little informal conversation will put both of you more at ease and help you build a better relationship

4. After you have completed your evaluation, ask for your employee's opinion. Your Latino employee will welcome the opportunity to share ideas with you.

After you study this section of vocabulary, review your company's evaluation form. What words from this chapter could help you? Start a form in Spanish to help you prepare for these important conferences.

> Don't let your desk become a barrier for good communications. Get up and sit beside your employee. If that's not possible because of the furniture arrangement in your office, move your chair beside your desk or in front of it.

English	Español	Guide
It's…!	¡Es…!	es
Excellent	Excelente	x-see-**LEN**-tay
Fantastic	Fantástico	fan-**TAS**-t-co
Good	Bueno	boo-**WAY**-no
What good work!	¡Qué buen trabajo!	kay boo-**WAYNE** tra-**BAA**-ho
Very good!	¡Muy bien!	mooy BN
You're very important!	¡Usted es muy importante!	oo-**STED** es mooy m-por-**TAN**-tay
You learn quickly.	Aprende rápido.	ah-**PREN**-day **RAH**-p-doe
I respect you.	Le respeto.	lay race-**PAY**-toe
You are very valuable.	¡Usted es valioso!	oo-**STED** es val-ee-**OH**-so
There is/are…	Hay…	eye
Opportunity	Oportunidad	oh-por-too-knee-**DAD**
Great potential	Gran potencial	gran po-ten-see-**AL**
Obvious progress	Progreso obvio	pro-**GRES**-oh **OB**-v-oh
Positive feedback	Reacción positiva	ray-ax-see-**ON** po-see-**T**-va
Realistic goals	Metas posibles	**MAY**-tas po-**SEE**-blays

Tips and Tidbits

Two core cultural values to Latin Americans are "*respeto*" and "*personalismo*." Both are important in business settings. A professional in almost any endeavor is respected. He or she is treated with the courtesy because of the high degree of education they have achieved or their position within in an organization. Age is also an important factor in "*respeto*."

Meals and Beverages

Let's move on to restaurant basics, starting with meals and beverages. In the next chapters you will learn vocabulary for all sorts of items found in the kitchen, pantry and at the table. We are going to start with basic food groups and move on to kitchen machines, cleaning items, table settings and a whole range of action words.

To help you learn this vocabulary, think about the foods you like or what you prepare in your restaurant.

Choose the word for a meal like breakfast and see how many foods you can name that would commonly be associated with that meal.

English	Español	Guide
Meal	Comida	co-**ME**-da
Appetizer	Tapas	**TA**-pas
Breakfast	Desayuno	day-say-**UNO**
Lunch	Almuerzo	al-moo-**AIR**-so
Dinner	Cena	**SAY**-na
Dessert	Postre	**POS**-tray
Beer	Cerveza	ser-**VAY**-sa
Coffee	Café	ca-**FAY**
Decaffeinated coffee	Café descafeinado	ca-**FAY** des-ca-fay-**NA**-doe
Diet soda	Refresco dieta	ray-**FRAYS**-co d-**EH**-ta
Ice	Hielo	ee-**A**-low
Iced tea	Té helado	tay a-**LA**-doe
Juice	Jugo	**WHO**-go
Lemonade	Limonada	lee-mon-**NA**-da

English	Español	Guide
Milkshake	Batido	ba-**TEE**-doe
Red wine	Vino tinto	**V**-no **TEEN**-toe
Salad	Ensalada	n-sa-**LA**-da
Sandwich	Sándwich	sandwich
Snack	Merienda	may-ree-**N**-da
Soft drink	Refresco Soda	ray-**FRES**-co **SO**-da
Soup	Sopa	**SO**-pa
Tea	Té	tay
Water	Agua	**AH**-goo-ah
White wine	Vino blanco	**V**-no **BLAN**-co
Wine	Vino	**V**-no

Para Practicar

1. Which beverages do you associate with breakfast?

   _____

2. Which beverages do you associate with "happy hour"?

   _____

3. Name a beverage which contains no calories. _____

4. Name a beverage made with ice-cream. _____

Tips and Tidbits

Many Latin Americans begin the day with a *pan dulce* (sweet bread) and cup of coffee for breakfast. This interesting bread can assume many flavors. In spite of its name, a *pan dulce* usually isn't very sweet— especially by American standards like the donut. *Pan dulce* is baked instead of fried, contains very little sugar and is often flavored with a hint of cinnamon. ¡Fantástico!

In the Kitchen
En la Cocina

The kitchen is a very busy place where everyone works as a team to take care of customers and to take care of each other by working safely. This presents serious challenges when many on your staff speak *inglés* and others speak *español*. It's critical that everyone understands the importance of filling orders fast, while following safety precautions to prevent on-the-job accidents. No matter what happens in the kitchen, sanitation standards must be maintained. After all, it doesn't matter how good the food is or how good it looks, if the kitchen is dirty!

In this list, you will find terms for items found in and around the kitchen area. It is a long and detailed list, but don't let it overwhelm you. *¡No se preocupe!* Don't worry! Learning Spanish is like eating a big, juicy steak. You can't possibly eat the whole thing in one big gulp. You would choke! The same principle applies to learning a new language. Take small bites of Spanish. Enjoy each tasty morsel and get the full flavor from it before you go on to the next bite. Simply relax and enjoy it!

There's also another added benefit to learning slowly. By working slowly on your vocabulary and other skills, you remember them longer.

Try learning ten words each week and have fun! First, go over the list and highlight the ten words that you will use most. Those are the words you should start learning first. Don't waste time on terms that you won't use. You won't remember them. After you have mastered your first ten words, go on to the next set.

Only you know when you're ready to move on to new territory. If possible, label items around your workplace and find a practice partner. There is probably someone on your staff who speaks *español*. They will be glad to help you. Working with a partner will keep you focused — and you'll have more fun!

English	Español	Guide
Apron	Delantal	day-lan-TAL
Baking pan	Cacerola de hornear	cah-say-ROLL-ah day or-nay-are
Banquet	Banquete	ban-KET-tay
Bottle	Botella	bow-TAY-ya
Bottle opener	Destapador	des-ta-pa-DOOR
Bread warmer	Calentador de pan	cal-len-ta-DOOR day pan
Buffet	Buffet	boo-FAY
Bus tub	Cubeta	coo-BAY-ta
Bus person	Ayudante de mesero	eye-u-DAN-tay day may-SAY-row
Burner	Quemador	kay-ma-DOOR
Cake pan	Cacerola de tartas	ca-say-ROLL-ah day TAR-tas
Can	Lata	LA-ta
Can opener	Abrelatas	AH-bray-LA-tas
Chef	Jefe de cocina	HEF-a day Co-SEEN-na
China	Loza	LOW-sa
Coffee grinder	Molino de café	mo-LEE-no day Ca-FAY
Coffee maker	Cafetera	ca-fay-TER-ra
Coffee pot	Jarra para café	HAR-rah PA-rah ca-FAY
Coffee warmer	Plato caliente	PLA-toe cal-lee-N-tay
Colander	Colador	co-la-DOOR
Condiments	Aderezos	ah-day-RAY-sos
Crumbs	Migajas	me-GA-has

English	Español	Guide
Cutting board	Tabla de cortar	TA-bla day core-TAR
Dessert cart	Carro de postres	CAR-row day POST-rays
Dining room	Comedor	co-may-DOOR
Dishes	Vajillas	va-HE-yas
Dishwasher	Lavaplatos	la-va-PLA-toes
Dishwasher rack	Rejilla	ray-HE-ya
Dough	Masa	MA-sa
Filter	Filtro	FEEL-tro
Food and beverage	Comidas y bebidas	co-ME-das e bay-BEE-das
Frying pan	Sartén	sar-TEN
Garnish	Guarnición	goo-are-knee-see-ON
Grater	Rallador	rah-ya-DOOR
Half sheet pan	Media bandeja	MAY-dee-ah ban-DAY-ja
Hot water	Agua caliente	AH-goo-ah ca-lee-N-tay
Ice	Hielo	e-YEA-low
Ice bucket	Hielera	ee-ay-LAIR-rah
Ice cubes	Cubitos de hielo	Coo-BEE-toes day e-YEA-low
Kettle	Marmita	mar-ME-ta
Kitchen	Cocina	co-SEE-na
Lid	Tapadera	ta-pa-DARE-rah
Menu item	Platillo	pla-TEE-yo
Microwave oven	Microondas	me-crow-UN-das
Mixer	Batidora	ba-t-DOOR-rah

English	Español	Guide
Name tag	Placa de nombre	**PLA**-ca day **NOM**-bray
Napery	Mantelería	man-tail-lair-**REE**-ah
Napkin holder	Servilletero	ser-v-lay-**TAY**-row
Pan	Cacerola	ca-say-**ROLL**-ah
Pantry	Despensa	des-**PEN**-sa
Paper	Papel	**PA**-pel
Pie pan	Cacerola de pastel	ca-say-**ROLL**-ah day pas-**TELL**
Requisition	Pedido	pay-**DEE**-doe
Roasting pan	Cacerola de asado	ca-say-**ROLL**-ah day ah-**SA**-doe
Rolling pin	Rodillo	row-**DEE**-yo
Room set-up	Preparación del salón	pray-pa-rah-see-**ON** del sa-**LOAN**
Sauté pan	Cacerola de sauté	ca-say-**ROLL**-ah day saw-**TAY**
Self-service	Autoservicio	ow-toe-ser-**V**-see-oh
Service station	Aparador	ah-pa-ra-**DOOR**
Service table	Mesa de servicio	**MAY**-sa day ser-**V**-see-**OH**
Sheet pan	Bandeja	ban-**DAY**-ha
Shelf	Estante	es-**TAN**-tay
Sink	Fregadero	fray-ga-**DARE**-row
Skimmer	Espumadera	es-poo-ma-**DAY**-rah
Spatula	Espátula	es-**PA**-too-la
Sponge	Esponja	es-**PONE**-ha
Spoon (large)	Cuchara grande	coo-**CHA**-rah **GRAN**-day

English	Español	Guide
Spoon (small)	Cuchara pequeño	coo-**CHA**-rah pay-**CANE**-yo
Soda dispenser	Máquina de refrescos	**MA**-key-na day ray-**FRAYS**-cos
Stem/handle	Mango	**MAN**-go
Storeroom	Almacén	al-ma-**SEN**
Strainer	Colador	co-la-**DOOR**
To go box	Caja para llevar	**CA**-ha **PA**-rah yea-**VARE**
To-go cup	Vaso para llevar	**VA**-so **PA**-rah yea-**VARE**
Tongs	Pinzas	**PEEN**-sas
Tray	Charola	cha-**ROLL**-la
	Bandeja	ban-**DAY**-ha
Tray stand	Tijeras	tee-**HAIR**-rahs
Uniform	Uniforme	oon-knee-**FORM**-may
Wire whip	Batidor	ba-tee-**DOOR**

Tips and Tidbits

¡Ten paciencia! Have patience! On any work day managers give instructions to team members at a fast pace. The next time you are in this situation, look at your staff carefully. Are your Spanish-speaking team members nodding their heads as if they understand your instructions? To nod agreement is often a defense mechanize that is very cultural in the Latino work place. Employees want to tell "*el jefe*" or the boss what he or she wants to hear — and you want to hear that you've been understood. Remember that non-native speakers are translating what you are saying back into their native language, and that takes time. Also, when possible, pair demonstrations with verbal instructions. Often the brain processes body language faster than it does words!

Action in the Restaurant
Acción en el restaurante

Giving instructions to Spanish-speaking employees can be easier than you think. The following is a list of action words or verbs that are commonly used in and around restaurants. In order to make a request, start your sentence with "*favor de*" (fa-VOR-day) then add one of the verbs from the list. This takes on the automatic meaning of "please" and adds the instruction you want to. It's very polite— and it's a very quick way to get the results you need.

English	Español	Guide
To boil	Hervir	air-VEER
To bread	Empañar	m-pan-YAR
To chop meat	Trocear	tro-say-ARE
To chop vegetables	Picar	pee-CAR
To clear the table	Retirar el servicio usado	ray-teer-RAR l ser-VEE-see-oh oo-SA-doe
To cover	Cubrir	coob-REAR
To defrost	Descongelar	des-con-hell-ARE
To empty or drain	Vaciar	va-see-ARE
To dry	Secar	say-CAR
To eat	Comer	co-MARE
To fry	Freír	fray-EAR
To grill	Asar	ah-SAR
To mince/grind	Picar	pee-CAR
To mix	Mezclar	mays-CLAR
To peel	Pelar	pay-LAR
To plate	Emplatar	m-pla-TAR
To poach	Hervir a fuego lento	air-VEER ah foo-A-go LEN-toe

English	Español	Guide
To refill	Rellenar	ray-yea-**NAR**
To rinse	Aclarar	ah-clah-**RAHER**
To roast	Asar	ah-**SAR**
To sauté	Saltear	sal-tay-**ARE**
To serve	Servir	ser-**VEER**
To set the table	Poner la mesa	po-**NAIR** la **MAY**-sa
To slice	Rebanar	ray-baa-**NAR**
To smoke	Fumar	foo-**MAR**
To separate	Separar	say-pa-**RAR**
To spill	Derramar	day-rah-**MAR**
To stock	Surtir	soor-**TEAR**
To take the order	Tomar el orden	toe-**MAR** l **OR**-den
To toast	Tostar	toe-**STAR**
To towel dry	Secar con trapo	say-**CAR** con **TRAH**-poe
To wrap	Envolver	n-vol-**VAIR**

Kitchen Machines
Máquinas de la Cocina

As you begin learning the words for the machines you use in the kitchen, some of them will seem familiar. Why? That's because there's a strong relationship between many of these nouns and the verbs you learned in the last chapter. Here's an example: to freeze is "*congelar*" and the word freezer is "*congelador*." Only the last few letters are different in each word. This strong relationship between these two important parts of speech makes learning this list of vocabulary much easier. Look through the list and find as many similarities as you can with the verbs in the preceding section before you begin putting them in priority order.

English	Español	Guide
Broiler/grill	Parilla	pa-**REE**-ya
Can opener	Abrelatas	ah-bray-**LA**-tas
Coffee maker	Cafetera	ka-fay-**TER**-ah
Deep fryer	Freidora	fray-ee-**DOOR**-ah
Dish washer	Lavaplatos	**LA**-va-**PLA**-toes
Freezer	Congelador	con-hel-ah-**DOOR**
Griddle	Plancha	**PLAN**-cha
Milk dispenser	Surtidor de leche	soor-tee-**DOOR** day **LAY**-che
Mixer	Batidora	Ba-tee-**DOOR**-rah
Oven	Horno	**OR**-no
Refrigerator	Refrigerador	ray-free-hair-ah-**DOOR**
Soap dispenser	Distribuidor de jabón	dees-tree-boo-ee-**DOOR** day ha-**BON**
Sprayer	Rociador	row-cee-ah-**DOOR**
Steamer	Marmita al vapor	mare-**ME**-ta al va-**POUR**
Toaster	Tostadora	toe-sta-**DOOR**-rah
Walk-in freezer	Cámara congeladora	**CA**-ma-rah con-hell-la-**DOOR**-rah
Walk-in refrigerator	Cámara fría	**CA**-ma-rah **FREE**-ah

Para Practicar

1. Name the appliances used for food storage.

2. Name the appliances which keep food cold.

3. Name items used in clean-up.

I'm Hungry!
¡Tengo hambre!

Now that you are expanding your vocabulary by learning the terms for items in and around your workplace, it's time to move up to the next level: foods. Each of the following sections is broken down by category. We'll start with restaurant staples like meats, fruits, and vegetables. In later chapters we'll move on to methods of food preparation, flavorings and measurements. For section of vocabulary always personalize what you learn to match your unique situation.

Meats and Seafood

English	Español	Guide
Meat	Carne	CAR-nay
Rare	Poco cocida	PO-co co-SEE-da
Medium	Medio cocida	MAY-d-oh co-SEE-da
Well-done	Bien cocida	b-N co-SEE-da
Bacon	Tocino	to-SEE-no
Beef	Carne de vaca	CAR-nay day VA-ca
Broth	Caldo	CAL-doe
Chicken	Pollo	POE-yo
Clam	Almeja	al-MAY-ha
Crab	Cangrejo	can-GREY-ho
Fish	Pescado	pace-KA-doe
Ground beef	Carne molida	CAR-nay mo-LEE-da
Ham	Jamón	ha-MON

English	Español	Guide
Hamburger	Hamburguesa	am-burr-**GAY**-sa
Hot Dog	Perro caliente	**PAY**-row ca-lee-**N**-tay
Lamb	Cordero	core-**DAY**-row
Liver	Hígado	**E**-ga-doe
Lobster	Langosta	lan-**GO**-sta
Meatball	Albóndiga	al-**BONE**-dee-ga
Oyster	Ostra	**OH**-stra
Pork	Cerdo	**SER**-doe
Pork chop	Chuleta de puerco	chew-**LAY**-ta day poo-**AIR**-co
Poultry	Carne de ave	**CAR**-nay day **AH**-vay
Roast beef	Rosbif	ros-**BEEF**
Sausage	Salchicha	sal-**CHI**-cha
	Chorizo	chore-**REE**-so
Scallops	Vieira	v-ay-**E**-rah
Seafood	Mariscos	ma-**REES**-cos
Shrimp	Camarón	ca-ma-**RON**
Steak	Bistec	**BEE**-stek
Stew	Guiso	goo-**E**-so
Tuna	Atún	ah-**TOON**
Turkey	Pavo	**PA**-vo
Veal	Ternera	ter-**NAY**-rah

Para Practicar:

1. List five of your favorite meats: _____
   _____
   _____

2. How do you like your steak to be prepared: _____

3. List three of your favorite seafoods: _____
   _____

4. List meats that you do not like or have never tried: _____
   _____

5. List all the poultry: _____
   _____

6. Which meats could you order at fast-food restaurants? _____
   _____

7. Which meats are pork products? _____

Tips and Tidbits

Hispanic tastes in foods and beverages are influencing the items we see on supermarket shelves. As a result, tropical fruit and vegetable varieties are much easier to find, and selections in the "ethnic" aisle are growing. A recent on-line study of the Hispanic population's taste preferences in beverages and sweets found that a high percentage preferred fruit flavors. Latinos tend to enjoy fruit-flavored sodas over colas. Here is a list of the most popular fruit flavors: Pineapple, mango, watermelon, strawberry, citrus and grape. The next time you go shopping, visit the ethnic aisle in your market and pick up a fruit-flavored soda. The flavor selection may surprise you. Chances are you'll find these unusual beverages to be a refreshing change of pace!

Fruits

You'll find several words with strong similarities in this list of tasty vocabulary. To help you learn them, the next time you visit a grocery store take your list of fruits with you to the produce section. As you look through the displays, how many of the fruits can you name? If you don't remember the word for a particular fruit, buy one. Take it home and take a bite.

Here's another fun suggestion for learning this vocabulary. Buy a variety of fruits and make a fruit basket. Using sticky notes label each fruit in your display with Spanish on the front side of the card and the English translation on the back. When you learn one of the new vocabulary words, reward yourself by eating the fruit. What a delicious way to learn!

English	Español	Guide
Fruit	Fruta	**FRU**-ta
Apple	Manzana	man-**SAN**-na
Apricot	Durazno	doo-**RAHS**-no
Banana	Plátano	**PLA**-ta-no
Blackberry	Mora	**MORE**-ah
Blueberry	Arándano	ah-**RAN**-da-no
Cantaloupe	Melón Cantalupo	may-**LOAN** can-ta-**LOO**-poe
Cherry	Cereza	say-**RAY**-sa
Coconut	Coco	**CO**-co
Fig	Higo	**E**-go
Grape	Uva	**OO**-va
Grapefruit	Toronja	toe-**ROAN**-ha
Lemon	Limón	lee-**MON**

English	Español	Guide
Lime	Lima	**LEE**-ma
Mango	Mango	**MAN**-go
Orange	Naranja	na-**RAN**-ha
Papaya	Papaya	pa-**PIE**-ya
Peach	Durazno	doo-**RAZ**-no
Pear	Pera	**PAY**-rah
Pineapple	Piña	**PEEN**-ya
Plum	Ciruela	see-roo-**A**-la
Prune	Ciruela pasa	see-roo-**A**-la **PA**-sa
Raisin	Pasita	pa-**SEE**-ta
Strawberry	Fresa	**FRAY**-sa
Tamarind	Tamarindo	ta-ma-**REEN**-doe
Watermelon	Sandía	san-**DEE**-ah

Tips and Tidbits

Bananas, Plantains and Plátanos— Bananas are one of the world's most popular fruits, but did you know that technically the banana is an herb? Because of its large size and structure, it is often mistaken for a tree; however it is in the genus Musa. Bananas grow in clusters called *hands* which contain approximately 20 individual fruits. Worldwide bananas are one of our most commonly eaten foods. Bananas rank fourth after rice, wheat and corn in human consumption. They are more than 23 different varieties which are grown in 130 countries, Bananas and *plantains* are closely related but are quite different in taste and texture. Plantains are hard, starchy bananas that are cooked throughout Latin America. They are never eaten raw. In the 1500s Spaniard, who saw a similarity to the plane tree that grows in Spain, gave the plantain its Spanish name *plátano*.

Vegetables

Now that you've mastered meats and fruits, let's toss some veggies into the mix. Many of the words on this list are similar between our languages like asparagus and *espárragos*, but you will see subtle differences in several others. Pay careful attention to words like corn on the cob or *elote* and green bean "*ejote*". One letter makes all the difference.

Note: Hispanics tend to eat more fresh fruits and vegetables than other segments of the population.

English	Español	Guide
Vegetables	Vegetales	vay-he-**TA**-lace
Artichoke	Alcachofa	al-ca-**CHO**-fa
Asparagus	Espárragos	ace-**PA**-rah-gos
Avocado	Aguacate	agua-**CA**-tay
Dried beans	Frijoles	free-**HO**-lace
Beet	Betabel	bay-ta-**BELL**
Black beans	Frijoles negros	free-**HO**-lace **NAY**-grows
Broccoli	Brócoli	**BRO**-co-lee
Brussels sprouts	Col de Bruselas	col day brew-**SAY**-las
Cabbage	Col	col
Carrot	Zanahoria	sa-na-**OR**-ree-ah
Cauliflower	Coliflor	co-lee-**FLOOR**
Celery	Apio	**AH**-p-oh
Corn	Maíz	ma-**EES**
Corn on the cob	Elote	a-**LOW**-tay

English	Español	Guide
Cucumber	Pepino	pay-**P**-no
Green bean	Ejote	a-**HOE**-tay
Green bell pepper	Pimiento verde	p-me-**N**-toe **VER**-day
Green peas	Guisantes	gee-**SAN**-tays
Leek	Puerro	poo-**A**-row
Lettuce	Lechuga	lay-**CHEW**-ga
Mushroom	Champiñón	cham-peen-**YON**
Onion	Cebolla	say-**BOY**-ya
Pea	Guisante	goo-ee-**SAN**-tay
Pepper	Pimiento	p-me-**N**-toe
Potato	Patata	pa-**TA**-ta
Pumpkin	Calabaza	ca-la-**BA**-sa
Squash	Calabacera	ca-la-ba-**SER**-rah
Sweet potato	Camote	ca-**MO**-tay
Tomato	Tomate	to-**MA**-tay
Zucchini	Calabacita verde	ca-la-ba-**SEE**-ta **VER**-day

Para Practicar

1. Name the ingredients you would put into a tossed green salad.

2. Which vegetable is your least favorite?

3. Name three of your favorite vegetables?

4. Which vegetables could you add to "stir-fried" Chinese dishes?

5. Name the ingredients that one generally finds in salsa.

Dairy and Egg Products

Dairy products and eggs are dietary staples around the world. No matter where you travel or live, you'll be amazed at the variety of mouth-watering dishes that involve these two culinary giants. Both are great sources of protein, and literally the basis of millions of recipes. Two world-class Latin American dishes come to mind in this category: Tres Leches Cake and Huevos Rancheros.

Tres Leches Cake or "three milk cake" is exactly what the name describes. It's a rich, butter cake soaked in three different milks: sweetened condensed milk, evaporated milk and whole milk or heavy cream. Combining the three milks provides just the right sweetness and moistness. Some carry the milk theme even farther by serving Tres Leches Cake with a coconut milk or goat's milk and caramel sauce. What a way to end a memorable meal!

Huevos Rancheros means "rancher's eggs" or "ranch-styled" eggs, and there are many different ways to prepare it. Some recipes call for beans and cheese, but traditionally, the dish consists of fried eggs served on tortillas with a spicy tomato-chile salsa on the side. Huevos Rancheros got its name in Mexico where it was served as a second breakfast to ranch hands after they finished morning chores. Now, it's not just for breakfast anymore and can also be served for a quick brunch or supper.

English	Español	Guide
Dairy Products	Productos Lácteos	pro-DUKE-toes LACK-tay-ohs
2% milk	Leche de dos por ciento	LAY-che day dose pour see-N-toe
Butter	Mantequilla	man-tay-KEY-ya
Butter milk	Suero	sue-A-row
Cheese	Queso	KAY-so

English	Español	Guide
Chocolate milk	Leche de chocolate	LAY-che day cho-ko-LA-tay
Cottage cheese	Requesón	ray-kay-SEWN
Cream	Crema	CRAY-ma
Cream cheese	Queso crema	KAY-so CRAY-ma
Egg	Huevo	oo-WAVE-oh
Egg white	Clara de huevo	CLA-rah day oo-WAVE-oh
Egg yolk	Yema de huevo	YEA-ma day oo-WAVE-oh
Evaporated milk	Leche evaporada	LAY-che a-vah-poor-RAH-da
Half and half	Leche con crema	LAY-che con CRAY-ma
Hard-boiled egg	Huevo duro	oo-WAVE-oh DO-row
Ice-cream	Helado	a-LA-doe
Margarine	Margarina	mar-gar-E-na
Milk	Leche	LAY-che
Non-fat milk	Leche sin grasa	LAY-che seen GRA-sa
Omelet	Tortilla de huevos	tor-T-ya day oo-WAVE-ohs
Parmesan cheese	Queso parmesano	KAY-so par-may-SAN-no
Scrambled egg	Huevo revuelto	oo-WAVE-oh ray-voo-L-toe
Soft boiled egg	Huevo pasado por agua	oo-WAVE-oh pa-SA-doe poor AH-goo-ah

English	Español	Guide
Sour cream	Crema de leche agria	CRAY-ma day LAY-che ah-GREE-ah
Sunny-side up	Yema blanda	YEA-ma BLAN-da
Sweetened condensed milk	Leche condensada	LAY-che con-den-SA-da
Whole milk	Leche entera	LAY-che enn-TAY-rah
Yogurt	Yogurt	yo-GOOR

Breads, Pasta, Desserts and More

Breads, pastas and desserts are becoming more varied as Latin American cooking is influenced by other cultures. Every major city throughout the Americas will have at least one bakery featuring French bread, *pan dulce* (sweet bread) or pizza dough, but flat breads, such as tortillas and "pocket-breads" like pitas, are considered kitchen staples. Traditionally, tortillas are made from corn, but wheat varieties also exist. Some restaurants and bakeries still make them by hand, the old-fashioned way. There's really nothing like the taste of a freshly grilled tortilla.

For centuries tacos and tamales have made great "to go" foods.

Chocolate is another important food with Latin American ties. It was discovered more than 2,000 years ago by ancient Mesoamericans in the tropical rainforests of the Americas. Aztecs and Mayans were among the first ancient peoples to use and enjoy chocolate. Chocolate was different in those days because it wasn't sweetened. Ground and mixed with other spices, it was made into a frothy, slightly bitter beverage. Legend has it that only Aztec kings, priests and decorated soldiers were allowed to drink this "hot chocolate." When the Spanish arrived in the Americas, they were introduced to the magical mixture and quickly took it back to Spain. Eventually, sugar and milk were added and the rest is history!

English	Español	Guide
Bread	Pan	Pahn
Cake	Tarta (large)	**TAR**-ta
	Pastel (small)	pas-**TELL**
Candy	Dulce	**DOOL**-say
Cereal	Cereal	say-ray-**AL**
Chips	Tostaditas	tos-ta-**D**-tas
Chocolate	Chocolate	cho-co-**LA**-tay
Cookie	Galleta	ga-**YEA**-ta
Cracker	Galleta salada	ga-**YEA**-ta sa-**LA**-da
Cupcake	Pastelito	pas-tay-**LEE**-toe
Custard	Flan	flahn
Honey	Miel	mee-**L**
Ice cream	Helado	a-**LA**-doe
Jam	Mermelada	mer-may-**LA**-da
Macaroni	Macarrones	ma-ca-**RONE**-ace
Noodles	Fideos	fe-**DAY**-ohs
Nut	Nuez	new-**ACE**
Oatmeal	Avena	ah-**VAY**-na
Pancakes	Panqueques	pan-**KAY**-kays
Pastry	Pastelería	pas-tell-lay-**REE**-ah
Peanut butter	Crema de cacahuate	**CRAY**-ma day ca-ca-who-**A**-tay
Pie	Pastel	pas-**TELL**
Pudding	Pudín	poo-**DEAN**
Rice	Arroz	ah-**ROHS**

English	Español	Guide
Rolls	Panecillos	pan-nay-**SEE**-yos
Sorbet	Sorbete	sor-**BAY**-tay
Spaghetti	Espagueti	ace-pa-**GAY**-tee
Toast	Pan tostado	pahn toes-**TA**-doe
Whole grain bread	Pan integral	pahn een-tay-**GRAL**

Cooking Methods

Latin American cooking methods vary from country to country, but one thing is certain; many Latinos are looking for healthier ways to prepare their favorite foods. Even though there hasn't been a rush of "fat-free" or sugar-free foods making their way into the ethnic food section of the grocery store, it's only a matter of time. Some tortilla chips; however, are now available in a lighter form, and after all, salsa is only a mixture of tomatoes and fresh vegetables. In moderation, this makes a tasty, south-of-the-border treat. Americans eat so much salsa every year that more of it is sold now than catsup!

English	Español	Guide
Baked	Al orno	al **OR**-no
Bitter	Amargo	ah-**MAR**-go
Boiled	Hervido	air-**V**-doe
Breaded	Empanado	m-pa-**NA**-doe
Broiled	Asado	ah-**SA**-doe
Chopped	Picado	pee-**CA**-doe
Cooked	Cocido	co-**SEE**-doe
Dry	Seco	**SAY**-co

English	Español	Guide
Fat-free	Sin grasa	seen **GRA**-sa
Fresh	Fresco	**FRAYS**-co
Fried	Frito	**FREE**-toe
Frozen	Congelado	con-hey-**LA**-doe
Grilled	A la parilla	ah la par-**E**-ya
Microwaved	Cocido en microondas	co-**SEE**-doe n me-crow-**OON**-das
Peeled	Pelado	pay-**LA**-doe
Raw	Crudo	**CREW**-doe
Ripe	Maduro	ma-**DOO**-row
Roasted	Asado	ah-**SA**-doe
Rotten	Podrido	poe-**DREE**-do
Salty	Salado	sa-**LA**-doe
Sautéed	Salteado	sal-tay-**AH**-doe
Sliced	Rebanado	ray-ba-**NA**-doe
Sour	Agrio	ah-**GREE**-oh
Spicy	Picante	pee-**CAHN**-tay
Steamed	Cocido al vapor	co-**SEE**-doe al va-**POOR**
Stewed	Guisado	gee-**SA**-doe
Sweet	Dulce	**DOOL**-say

Flavors and Ingredients

This list contains some of the most basic ingredients used in restaurant kitchens. Take a close look at the word for spice "especial." It is in a special category of Spanish words. Many words in English that begin with the letter "s" have amigos in Spanish that begin with the letter combination "es." These words are very easy to learn. Here are some examples:

Special	Especial
Study	Estudio
Stress	Estrés
Spice	Especia
Spaghetti	Espagueti

Which of these items does the pantry in your restaurant contain?

English	Español	Guide
Ingredients	Ingredientes	een-gray-dee-**N**-tays
Catsup	Catsup	**CAT**-soup
Cinnamon	Canela	ca-**NAY**-la
Garlic	Ajo	**AH**-ho
Herb	Hierba	e-**AIR**-bah
Mayonnaise	Mayonesa	ma-yo-**NAY**-sa
Mustard	Mostaza	mo-**STA**-sa
Oil	Aceite	ah-**SAY**-tay
Olive oil	Aceite de oliva	ah-**SAY**-tay day oh-**LEE**-va
Oregano	Orégano	oh-**RAY**-ga-no
Pepper	Pimienta	pee-me-**N**-ta
Salad dressing	Aderezo	ah-day-**RAY**-so
Salt	Sal	sal
Sauce	Salsa	**SAL**-sa
Spice	Especia	ace-**PAY**-see-ah
Sugar	Azúcar	ah-**SUE**-car
Vinegar	Vinagre	vee-**NAY**-gray

At the Table

Restaurant cutlery can be quite different from one establishment to another. Some restaurants feature elegant settings of fine china, while some find that paper plates and plastic cups fit the bill. Consequently, fine dining requires place settings that  are more elaborate, so the vocabulary in this setting will be more extensive than that found in family-style restaurants and cafés. The types of meals you serve in your restaurant dining room will determine the vocabulary you should learn. As you review the list below, think critically about the place setting your restaurant currently uses. Begin with a list of the things that every place setting has such as a plate, fork, knife, spoon, salt and pepper. Learn the basics first before proceeding into your specific area of restaurant operation.

English	Español	Guide
Ashtray	Cenicero	sen-knee-**SAY**-row
Beverage	Bebida	bay-**B**-da
Base plate	Plato base	**PLA**-toe **BAH**-say
Bill	Cuenta	coo-**AIN**-ta
Bowl	Tazón	ta-**SEWN**
Bread basket	Cesta para pan	**SAYS**-ta **PA**-rah pan
Bread plate	Plato para pan	**PLA**-toe **PA**-rah pan
Chair	Silla	**SEE**-ya
Customer	Cliente	clee-**N**-tay
Creamer	Jarrita para leche	ha-**REE**-ta **PA**-rah **LAY**-chay
Cup	Taza	**TA**-sa
Dessert	Postre	**POS**-tray

English	Español	Guide
Dessert plate	Plato de postre	**PLA**-toe day **POS**-tray
Paper napkin	Servilleta de papel	ser-ve-**YEA**-ta day pa-**PELL**
Pepper shaker	Pimentero	pe-men-**TAY**-row
Place setting	Plaqué	pla-**KAY**
Fork	Tenedor	ten-nay-**DOOR**
Glass	Vaso	**VA**-so
Glassware	Cristalería	cre-sta-lair-**REE**-ah
High chair	Silla de niños	**SEE**-ya day **KNEE**-nyos
Knife	Cuchillo	coo-**CHEE**-yo
Menu	Menú	may-**NEW**
Napkin	Servilleta	ser-ve-**YEA**-ta
Salad	Ensalada	n-sal-**LA**-da
Salad fork	Tenedor de ensalada	ten-nay-**DOOR** day n-sa-**LA**-da
Salt shaker	Salero	sa-**LAY**-row
Saucer	Plato de café	**PLA**-toe day ca-**FAY**
Silverware	Cubertería	co-bear-tay-**REE**-ah
Soup	Sopa	**SO**-pa
Soup plate	Plato de sopa	**PLA**-toe **PA**-rah **SO**-pa
Soup spoon	Cuchara de sopa	coo-**CHA**-rah day **SO**-pa
Spoon	Cuchara	coo-**CHA**-rah
Sugar bowl	Azucarero	ah-sue-ca-**RAY**-row
Table	Mesa	**MAY**-sa

English	Español	Guide
Table cloth	Mantel	man-TEL
Teaspoon	Cucharilla	coo-cha-REE-ya
Tip	Propina	pro-P-na
Waiter/waitress	Mesero (*m*)	may-SAY-row
	Mesera (*f*)	may-SAY-rah
Water glass	Vaso para agua	VA-so PA-rah AH-goo-ah
Wine glass	Vaso para vino	VA-so PA-rah V-no
Wine list	Carta de vinos	CAR-ta day VEE-nos

Tips and Tidbits:

Some Like it Hot: Calor, Picante and Caliente: Spanish is a very precise language. Often a specific word or description will have a very exact usage. A simple word like "hot" in English has three different Spanish translations depending on the specific meaning implied. It sounds complicated, but it's not. Here are some simple guidelines for using these not so simple but common words that will keep you from getting hot under the collar!

Calor is the Spanish word to use talking about hot weather or to talk about yourself on a hot day.

Picante is the word to use when describing the taste of hot, spicy food like salsa.

Caliente is for things that are hot to the touch like a hot cup of coffee.

Para Practicar
List the items used in your restaurant's basic table setting:
_____
_____
_____

Measurements

Latin America uses the metric system for weights and measurements. Most recipes use ounces and grams instead of teaspoons or tablespoons. This won't be a difficult concept; however, if you are unsure of *los números*, this would be a good time to review. It's also important to point out that you are going to see a very familiar Spanish word in this section used in a different context. The word *peso* is most commonly used as the term for Mexican currency — but it is also the word for a pound.

English	Español	Guide
Clove of garlic	Diente de ajo	d-N-tay day AH-ho
Cold	Frío	FREE-oh
Cube	Cubo	COO-bow
Cup	Taza	TA-sa
Degrees	Grados	GRA-dose
Half	Media	MAY-d-ah
Hot	Caliente	ca-lee-N-tay
Less	Menos	MAY-nose
Liter	Litro	LEE-tro
Milliliter	Mililitro	me-lee-LEE-tro
More	Más	mas
Ounce	Onza	ON-sa
Pound	Peso	PAY-so
Quarter	Cuarto	coo-WAR-toe
Tablespoon	Cucharada	coo-cha-RAH-da
Teaspoon	Cucharadita	coo-cha-rah-D-ta

English	Español	Guide
Temperature	Temperatura	tem-pear-rah-**TOO**-rah
Third	Tercero	ter-**SAY**-row
Three quarters	Tres cuartos	trays coo-**WAR**-toes
Whole	Entero	n-**TAY**-row

Para Practicar

1. List the measurements in your favorite recipe.

2. List the safe temperatures for cooking beef, poultry and pork

Restaurant Inspections
Inspecciones del Restaurant

Your establishment will be visited by a restaurant inspector from your county or state on a regular basis. These important inspections will provide you with good information on your sanitation and service techniques. They will also provide you with data you can use in training programs. Making sure that everyone knows the principals of safe food storage and proper service temperatures will make every meal you serve a memorable one — for all the right reasons!

In Latin America health codes and restaurant inspection techniques vary widely from country to country. In some rural areas of Central and South America, there are no inspections at all! Prepare your employees for the *inspección* in advance, so they will be more comfortable with the process. Preparing your Spanish-speaking employees for the process will also be a big help to the inspector. Here are some words that will help the procedure go more smoothly.

English	Español	Guide
Inspector	Inspector	n-spec-TOR
	Inspectora	n-spec-TOR-rah
Inspection	Inspección	n-spec-see-ON
Animals	Animal	ah-knee-mal
Ceiling	Techo	TAY-cho
Clean	Limpia	LEEM-pee-ah
Clean clothes	Vestidos limpios	ves-TEE-does LEEM-p-ohs
Contamination	Contaminación	con-ta-me-na-see-ON
Cross contamination	Contaminación transversa	con-ta-me-na-see-ON trans-VER-sa
Dry foods	Alimentos secos	ah-lee-MEN-toes SAY-cos
Dryer	Secadora	say-ca-door-RAH
Employees	Empleados	m-play-AH-does
Floor	Piso	P-so
Fly	Mosca	MOS-ca
Food	Comida	co-ME-da
Garbage cans	Basurero	bah-sue-RARE-row
Hair net	Redecilla	ray-day-SEE-ya
Hand washing	Lavando los manos	la-VAN-doe los MA-nose
Hygiene	Higiene	e-he-N-nay
Infection	Infección	n-fec-see-ON
Insects	Insectos	en-SEC-toes
Labels	Etiqueta	ay-tee-KAY-ta
Lavatory	Baño	BAN-yo

English	Español	Guide
Light	Luz	loose
Plates	Platos	**PLA**-toes
Preparation	Preparación	pray-pa-rah-see-**ON**
Protection	Protección	pro-tec-see-**ON**
Rat	Rata	**RAH**-ta
Restroom (*public*)	Servicio	ser-**VEE**-see-oh
Roaches	Cucarachas	coo-ca-**RAH**-chas
Sanitized	Saneado	sa-nay-**A**-doe
Sick	Enfermo	n-**FAIR**-mo
Signs	Letrero	lay-**TRAY**-row
Soap	Jabón	ha-**BONE**
Spoilage	Putrefacción	poot-ray-fac-see-**ON**
Temperature	Temperatura	tem-pear-rah-**TO**-rah
Thermometer	Termómetro	ter-**MO**-may-tro
Towels	Toallas	toe-**EYE**-yas
Transportation	Transportación	trans-pour-ta-see-**ON**
Ventilation	Ventilación	ven-tee-la-see-**ON**
Violation	Violación	vee-oh-la-see-**ON**
Wall	Pared	pa-**RED**
Water	Agua	**AH**-gua

Para Practicar

1. Name the items needed for hand washing. _____

2. What temperatures are appropriate for refrigerated *pollo* and *bistec?*

Cleaning Products
Productos para Limpiar

More often than not, we call a cleaning product by its brand name, like Windex, Clorox and Kleenex. You can do the same thing in Spanish! A brand name in Spanish is a *marca del producto*. Try this when you're at a loss for words. I need or *necessito* el Clorox,® el Comet,® el SOS,® el Kleenex,® or el Palmolive®.

Here are some other important tips about names. The names of businesses, streets and products are never translated into Spanish. That makes it easy to ask for a Coke or a Big Mac anywhere! Around the world, most American product names just stay the same.

Here's another important tip. Don't try to change your name to something that sounds like a Spanish name. If you had Spanish classes in high school or college, your teacher probably gave you a Spanish name. In the real world things are different. You should be called by your own name in any workplace setting to decrease the chance of on-the-job accidents If someone calls you by a name that you aren't accustomed to hearing, it will take you much longer to respond. That's because it's not something you are accustomed to hearing. In the seconds it takes you to realize that someone is speaking to you, you risk being seriously injured. Just be who you are!

Please use   **Favor de usar …**

English	Español	Guide
Bacteria	Bacteria	bac-**TER**-ree-ah
Cleaning solution	Líquido limpiador	**LEE**-key-doe leem-p-ah-**DOOR**
Detergent	Detergente	day-ter-**HEN**-tay
Drain	Desagüe	des-**AH**-guway

English	Español	Guide
Dumpster	Vertedero	ver-tay-DARE-row
	Basurero	ba-sue-RARE-row
Fingernails	Uñas	OON-yas
Food scraps	Desperdicios	des-pear-d-SEE-ohs
Garbage	Basura	ba-SUE-rah
Garbage disposal	Triturador de basura	tree-tour-ra-DOOR day ba-SUE-rah
	Eliminación	a-lee-me-na-see-OH
	Molina de basura	mo-LEE-na day ba-SUE-rah
Grease trap	Trampa de grasa	**TRAM**-pa day **GRA**-sa
Hair net	Redecilla	ray-day-SEE-ya
Hygiene	Higiene	ee-he-N-nay
Mop	Trapeador	tra-pay-ah-DOOR
Mop wringer	Escurridor	es-coo-ree-DOOR
Paper towel	Toalla de papel	toe-AH-ya day pa-PELL
Rag	Trapo	TRA-po
Sanitation	Saneamiento	san-ay-ah-me-N-toe
Scrub pad	Estropajo	es-tro-PA-ho
Soap	Jabón	ha-BONE
Soapy water	Agua jabonosa	AH-guah ha-bow-NO-sa
Squeegee	Escobilla de goma	es-co-B-ya day GO-ma
To clean	Limpiar	leem-p-ARE

English	Español	Guide
To dust	Sacudir	sa-coo-**DEAR**
To mop	Trapear	trah-pay-**ARE**
To rinse	Enjuagar	n-who-ah-**GAR**
To sanitize	Sanear	sah-nay-**ARE**
To scrub	Restregar	rays-tray-**GAR**
To sweep	Barrer	baa-**RAIR**
To wash	Lavar	la-**VAR**
Urn cleaner	Limpiador de cafeteras	leem-p-ah-**DOOR** day ca-fay-**TER**-rahs

Tips and Tidbits

Many Latin Americans are skilled diplomats who are quite sensitive to the world around them. This is particularly true in the workplace. For Latinos, conversation is an important skill and discussions are often lively. Everyone will have an opinion and will want to share it. Expressing yourself with passion is the norm in Latin America and strong body language abounds. It could even appear to you that the discussion is taking a heated turn, but that happens infrequently on the job.

When disagreements do occur, striving to reach a consensus where there are no winners or losers is an important goal in any conflict involving Hispanic employees. In a group or even a family situation, important decisions are often made for the benefit of the group rather than for the individual. Most Hispanics see themselves as an integral part of a social network where the group is always more important than the individual

Saving face is so important that many Latinos are sensitive to criticism and take it personally— even on the job. Aren't we all? If you are a manager, it's essential that you realize this and make every effort to avoid situations which show your Latino employees in a less than positive light, especially in front of others.

In The Guest's Room

As you train the Spanish-speaking members of your housekeeping staff, here are the names of common items found in a hotel guest's room. Each hotel has its own cleaning and maintenance routine. Think about how the rooms on your property are maintained and the amenities they contain. This will assist you in prioritizing your vocabulary in this important area. To help everyone learn this essential vocabulary, label an empty room with sticky notes in English and Spanish. Urge members of your housekeeping team to go to that room and run through the vocabulary as often as possible. If it's not possible to label an actual guest's room, post five new words each week in both languages in your break room. Everyone will learn together. This is a super practice exercise for team-building and it sends a clear message to the entire staff about the importance of learning Spanish in a business setting.

I need to clean your room, please.
Necesito limpiar su cuarto, por favor.

English	Español	Guide
Air conditioning	Aire acondicionado	EYE-ray ah-con-dee-see-oh-NA-doe
Bath tub	Bañera	ban-YEA-rah
Bathroom	Baño	BAN-yo
Bed	Cama	CA-ma
Bed spread	Colcha	COAL-cha
Cabinet	Armario	arm-MARE-ree-oh
Chair	Silla	SEE-ya
Clock	Reloj	RAY-low
Closet	Armario	are-MAR-e-oh

English	Español	Guide
Curtain	Cortina	cor-**TEE**-na
Desk	Escritorio	es-cree-**TOR**-ree-oh
Door	Puerta	pooh-**AIR**-ta
Dust ruffle	Guardapolvo	goo-**ARE**-da-**POLE**-vo
Floor	Piso	**P**-so
Iron	Plancha	**PLAHN**-cha
Ironing board	Tabla de planchar	**TA**-blah de plan-**CHAR**
Lamp	Lámpara	**LAMB**-pa-rah
Light	Luz	loose
Mirror	Espejo	es-**PAY**-jo
Pillow	Almohada	al-mo-**HA**-da
Pillow case	Funda de almohada	**FOON**-da day al-mo-**HA**-da
Sheet	Sábano	**SA**-baa-no
Shower	Ducha	**DO**-cha
Sink	Lavabo	la-**VAH**-bow
Sofa	Sofá	so-**FA**
Table	Mesa	**MAY**-sa
Telephone	Teléfono	tay-**LAY**-foe-no
Television	Televisión	tay-lay-vee-see-**ON**
Trash	Basura	bah-**SUE**-rah
Towel	Toalla	toe-**EYE**-ya
Wall	Pared	pah-**RED**
Water	Agua	**AH**-gua
Window	Ventana	ven-**TAN**-na

Talking with the Housekeeping

Recently an associate told me about a situation he found himself in on a business trip. Early one morning a member of the hotel's housekeeping staff knocked at his  door. As she entered the room and began her cleaning routine, she said, "*Buenos días, señor.*" Mike, who is a savvy, environmentally conscious traveler, was staying at the hotel only one more day, so he didn't want the housekeeper to change the sheets. Seeing that Mike was trying to tell her something, the housekeeper, who didn't speak *inglés*, handed him a card on which the phrases below were written. Mike thought the phrases were so practical, he asked for a copy when he checked out. Since he shared them with us, we want to share them with you.

English	Español	Guide
Please clean the room.	Favor de limpiar la habitación.	fa-**VOR** day leem-p-**ARE** la ah-b-ta-see-**ON**
No service, please.	No servicio, por favor.	no ser-**V**-see-oh pour fa-**VOR**
Just trash	Sola basura	**SO**-la ba-**SUE**-rah
Just towels	Sola toallas	**SO**-la toe-**EYE**-yas
I need more regular coffee.	Necesito más café regular.	nay-say-**SEE**-toe mas ca-**FAY** ray-goo-**LAR**
I need more decaffeinated coffee.	Necesito más café descafeinado.	nay-say-**SEE**-toe mas ca-**FAY** des-ca-fee-**NA**-doe
Coffee in the green packet	Café en el paquete verde	ca-**FAY** in el pa-**KET**-tay **VER**-day
I need extra towels.	Necesito más toallas.	nay-say-**SEE**-toe mas toe-**EYE**-yas

English	Español	Guide
Change the sheets.	Cambie las sábanas.	**CAM**-be-a las **SA**-ba-nas
Clean the bathroom.	Limpie el baño.	**LEEM**-p-ay el **BAHN**-yo
Vacuum the room	Aspire la habitación.	ah-**SPHERE**-ay la ah-b-ta-see-**ON**
Come back later.	Regrese más tarde.	ray-**GRES**-ay mas **TAR**-day
In 10 minutes	En diez minutos	in d-**ACE** me-**NEW**-toes
In 30 minutes	En treinta minutos	in **TRAIN**-ta me-**NEW**-toes
In an hour	En una hora	in una **OR**-rah
I need more tissue.	Necesito más de papel Kleenex®.	nay-say-**SEE**-toe mas day pa-**PEL** Kleenex®
I need more shampoo.	Necesito más champú.	nay-say-**SEE**-toe mas cham-**POO**
I need more lotion	Necesito más cremas.	nay-say-**SEE**-toe mas **CRAY**-mas
I need more toilet paper	Necesito más papel de baño.	nay-say-**SEE**-toe mas pa-**PEL** day **BAHN**-yo
I need more soap	Necesito más jabones	nay-say-**SEE**-toe mas ja-**BOW**-nace
I need to talk to a supervisor.	Necesito hablar con un supervisor.	nay-say-**SEE**-toe ah-**BLAR** con sue sue-pear-**V**-soar
I would like	Me gustaría	me goo-sta-**REE**-ah

Tips and Tidbits
Brand names such as Kleenex® or Coca Cola® are not translated.

Around the Hotel
Alrededor del Hotel

Great resorts and hotels are full of interesting spaces for guests to enjoy. Many times attractions like golf and tennis are the reasons that guests choose these locations for relaxation or business conferences. Keeping the grounds in top shape requires working with a large numbers of trained professionals. How many of the following spots or items do you have on your property?

English	Español	Guide
Beach	Playa	**PLY**-ya
Courtyard	Patio	**PA**-tee-oh
Exit light	Luz de salida	loose day sa-**LEE**-da
Fire detector	Detector de fuego	day-tek-**TOR** day foo-**A**-go
Fountain	Fuente	foo-**N**- tay
Game room	Salón de juegos	sa-**LAWN** day who-**WAY**-goes
Garden	Jardín	har-**DEAN**
Garden path	Andador	an-da-**DOOR**
Golf course	Campo de golf	**CAM**-po day golf
Guest room	Habitación	ah-bee-ta-see-**ON**
Laundry	Lavandería	la-van-dare-**REE**-ah
Lawn	Césped Yarda	**SAYS**-ped **YAR**-da
Lobby	Vestíbulo	veh-**TEE**-boo-low
Maintenance shop	Taller	ta-**YER**

English	Español	Guide
Office	Oficina	oh-fee-**SEEN**-na
Parking lot	Estacionamiento	es-ta-see-on-a-me-**N**-toe
Pool	Piscina	p-**SEEN**-na
Restaurant	Restaurante	reh-stower-**RAHN**-tay
Smoke detector	Detector de humo	day-tec-**TOR** day **OO**-mo
Storeroom	Almacén	al-ma-**SIN**
Tennis court	Cancha de tenis	**CAN**-cha day **TAY**-knees

Para Practicar
1. Name items from the list above which are found in each guest room.
2. Name areas on your property which are for sports.
3. Name items on your property related to safety.

Tips & Tidbits
Employees with different cultural backgrounds will have different attitudes towards work and employers that will have an impact on your management style. According to Eva S. Kras in her book *Management in Two Cultures* (Intercultural Press, 1995) Latin Americans are less likely to report an on-the-job injury than American employees. In many areas south of the border workers are essentially trained to tell the boss what he *wants* to hear rather than what he *needs* to hear. Many Latin Americans fear that they will be fired if they become injured on the job— or if they are handling a piece of equipment that breaks. Training is the key to managing these issues. Use your Spanish to help you build open relationships that keep lines of communication open. Making sure that you know everyone's name and how to pronounce it correctly is a good start. In Latin America greeting individual employees is very important

Giving Directions

The ability to give directions in *español* is one of the most practical skills you can develop. As you direct employees or guests from one area of your property or restaurant, these words will really be a *grande* plus to your conversational ability. You will use these words over and over again. Slowly, you can start to learn this important vocabulary by knowing simple things, such as the four directions: north, south, east, and west. Next add turns like right and left. Before you know it, you'll be able to give directions to places around town and in your office. This practical vocabulary is easy to practice because you can work on it anywhere you go!

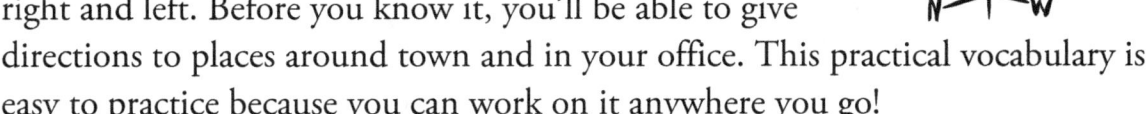

English	Español	Guide
Where is…?	¿Dónde está…?	**DON**-day es-**TA**
North	Norte	**NOR**-tay
South	Sur	**SUE**-er
East	Este	**ES**-tay
West	Oeste	oh-**ES**-tay
Above	Encima	n-**SEE**-ma
Aisle	Pasillo	pa-**SEE**-yo
Avenue	Avenida	ah-vay-**KNEE**-da
Behind	Detrás	day-**TRAHS**
Down	Abajo	ah-**BAA**-ho
Here	Aquí	ah-**KEY**
In front of	En frente de	n **FREN**-tay day
Inside	Adentro	ah-**DEN**-tro
Near	Cerca	**CER**-ca
Next to	Al lado de	al **LA**-doe day

English	Español	Guide
Outside	Afuera	ah-foo-**AIR**-ah
Over there	Allá	ah-**YA**
Straight ahead	Adelante	ah-day-**LAN**-tay
Street	Calle	ca-**YEA**
There	Allí	ah-**YE**
To the left	A la izquierda	ah la ees-key-**AIR**-dah
Turn	Doble	**DOE**-blay
To the right	A la derecha	ah la day-**RAY**-cha
Up	Arriba	ah-**REE**-ba

Tips & Tidbits:
Neither the names of businesses nor the names of streets are translated into Spanish. The proper name of your agency is its brand or trade-mark and should not be translated. Consequently, the name of a street is its proper or given name and should not be translated either.

In most Latin American cities, numbers and the words street and avenue are commonly used in addresses as they are in most metropolitan areas of the US. It's not uncommon to find 5th Avenue or 52nd Street. But, our neighborhood streets…well, that's another story entirely! Street names like Taniger Lane, Red Fox Run, or Wood Stork Cove are impossible to translate from one language to another. You should be aware; however, that sometimes a Spanish-speaking person will give you the number of their street address *en español.* Simple numbers are one of the most important sets of vocabulary you can have!

Around Town

Spanish-speaking families are traveling more and more for vacations. Family destinations like Orlando, Las Vegas and beach resorts are common choices. If you are working at the reception desk, guests will ask you a wide variety of questions. You need to know where restaurants are located, what transportation options are available and also be able to help with financial arrangements, just to name a few! When a Hispanic family checks in to your property, they will want to check out the surrounding area too. Knowing vocabulary for places around town will provide you with the kind of terminology that will make you a good ambassador for your area.

The next time you go out to run errands around your city or town, check the list below. Where are you going? Make a numbered list of the places you intend to go along with the Spanish words for the directions that will get you there. Now you can practice two important sets of vocabulary at the same time. Also think about grouping this vocabulary into logical sets. Which places involve travel? Which places involve recreation? Which locations do your guests ask you about most often? Now, let's get going!

English	Español	Guide
Airport	Aeropuerto	ah-eh-row-poo-**AIR**-toe
Bakery	Panadería	pan-ah-day-**REE**-ah
Bank	Banco	**BAN**-co
Barber shop	Peluquería	pay-loo-kay-**REE**-ah
Beauty salon	Salón de belleza	sa-**LAWN** day bay-**YEA**-sa
Church	Iglesia	e-**GLAY**-see-ah
City hall	Municipio	moon-knee-**SEE**-p-oh

English	Español	Guide
Fire department	Departamento de bomberos	day-par-ta-**MEN**-toe day bom-**BAY**-rows
Florist	Florería	floor-ray-**REE**-ah
Gas station	Gasolinera	gas-so-lee-**NAY**-rah
Grocery store	Grosería	gros-eh-**REE**-ah
Hospital	Hospital	os-p-**TAL**
Hotel	Hotel	oh-**TEL**
Jewelry store	Joyería	hoy-eh-**REE**-ah
Laundromat	Lavandería	la-van-day-**REE**-an
Library	Biblioteca	b-lee-oh-**TECK**-ah
Market	Mercado	mare-**CA**-doe
Movie theatre	Cine	**SEEN**-nay
Museum	Museo	moo-**SAY**-oh
Park	Parque	**PAR**-kay
Pharmacy	Farmacia	far-**MA**-see-ah
Police station	Estación de policía	es-ta-see-**ON** day po-lee-**SEE**-ah
Post office	Correo	core-**A**-oh
Restaurant	Restaurante	res-tower-**RAHN**-tay
School	Escuela	es-coo-**A**-la
Shoe store	Zapatería	sa-pa-tay-**REE**-ah
Store	Tienda	t-**N**-da
Super market	Super Mercado	soo-**PEAR** mare-**CA**-doe
Theatre	Teatro	tay-**AH**-trow
Train station	Estación de tren	es-ta-see-**ON** day tren

Landscaping & Irrigation

Beautiful landscaping is one of the features that guests will remember about your property. Whether you are maintaining a large resort or a small family-owned bed and breakfast, you will need many professionals to assist you. The following is a list of the most common tools or items used in landscaping and irrigation. Depending on your specialty, you may not need to learn each word listed. Go through the words and make a check-list of the vocabulary you use most often. Label your tools if possible so you can see the Spanish word more frequently.

One thing you will notice is that some of the items listed have more than one definition. It's common, especially with construction tools that an item will be called one thing in Mexico and go by a completely different name in another country. In the list below you will see that the word "drill" has two meanings listed. The first word listed is the most common and/or the easiest for an English-speaking person to remember. But, it's always a good idea to share your vocabulary with your Spanish-speaking crew to learn more about the words they use among themselves.

English	Español	Guide
Blower	Soplador	so-pla-**DOOR**
Chain	Cadena	ka-**DAY**-nah
Chain saw	Sierra cadena	see-**AIR**-ah ca-**DAY**-nah
Clippers	Cortadora	core-ta-**DOOR**-ah
Concrete block	Bloque de cemento	**BLO**-kay day say-**MEN**-toe
Container	Contenedor	con-ten-**A**-door
Diesel	Diesel	Same as English
Drill	Perfore	pear-**FOR**
	Taladro (tool)	ta-**LA**-drow

English	Español	Guide
Edger	Caladora	ca-la-**DOOR**-ah
Fertilizer	Fertilizante	fair-til-lee-**ZAN**-tay
Flowers	Flores	**FLOOR**-rays
Gas	Gasolina	gas-so-**LEE**-nah
Grease	Grasa	**GRA**-sa
Grease Gun	Pistola de grasa	p-**STOW**-la day **GRA**-sa
Hacksaw	Sierra para metales	see-**AIR**-ah **PA**-ra may-**TAL**-ace
Hose	Manguera	man-**GAY**-rah
Hose off or water	Regar	**RAY**-gar
Irrigation	Irrigación or riego	ear-ree-gah-see-**ON** ree-**A**-go
Knife	Cuchillo navaja *(utility)*	coo-**CHEE**-yo na-**VA**-ha
Level	Nivel *(tool)*	**KNEE**-vel
	Nivelar *(v)*	knee-vel-**ARE**
Manure	Abono	ah-**BOW**-no
Mattock	Pico	**PEE**-ko
Mulch	Pajote or	pah-**HO**-tay
	Cubrir con pajote	coo-**BREAR** kon pah-**HO**-tay
Nail	Clavo	**KLA**-vo
Oil	Aceite	ah-**SAY**-tay
Pine needles	Aguja de pino	ah-**GOO**-ha day **P**-no
Rake	Rastrillo	ras-**TREE**-yo
Seed	Semilla	say-**ME**-ya

English	Español	Guide
Shovel	Pala	**PAH**-la
Sod (yard)	Césped	**CES**-ped
Sod staples	Grapas de césped	**GRA**-pas day **CES**-ped
Sprayer	Pulverizador	pull-ver-ree-**SA**-door
Spreader	Propagador	pro-pah-**GA**-door
Straw	Paja	**PAH**-ha
Tamper	Pisón Apisonar (v)	pee-**SON** ah-pee-son-**ARE**
Tarp	Lona	**LOW**-na
Trailer	Transporte por camión	trans-**POR**-tay pour **CA**-me-**ON**
Tree	Árbol	**ARE**-bowl
Truck	Camión	**CA**-me-**ON**
Truck bed	Cama de camión	**CA**-ma day **KA**-me-**ON**
Truck cab	Interior de camión	en-tear-**REE**-or day ca-me-**ON**
Water tank	Tanque de agua	tan-**KAY** de **AH**-goo-ah
Weed	Mala hierba	**MA**-la e-**AIR**-bah
Weed eater	Escardadora	ace-car-dah-**DORA**
Weed killer	Herbicida	air-bee-**SEE**-da
Wheel	Rueda	roo-**A**-dah
Window	Ventana	ven-**TA**-na
Wrench	Llave	**YAH**-vay
Yard	Yarda (*Spanglish*) Césped	**YAR**-da ses-**PED**

One for the Road: Phrases to Use Any Time

Obviously, conversation is made up of more than just lists of words. It will take practice and determination for you to achieve free-flowing conversation in a language that's new to you. Learning Spanish is a slow and steady process for adults. It could take several months before you begin to "think" in Spanish, so don't expect to achieve native speaker speed overnight. There will be times when you feel like you can't remember anything you've studied. That's natural. It happens to everyone. Try not to be discouraged. The rewards you'll receive from learning to speak Spanish are far greater than a little bit of frustration. If you keep working, it won't be long before you'll have a breakthrough. Learning Spanish is a lot like eating a great steak. You don't want to rush it. Cut each bite of your Spanish, chew it over carefully, and savor each morsel. Moving along at a slower pace will help you retain what you learn longer.

Spanish is a language that has loads of zest and flair. It is punctuated with single words and short phrases that can really express a lot of sentiment. The next time you have an opportunity to observe native speakers, listen carefully. You may hear them switch from English to Spanish, depending on what they are saying. And, you might hear them use any of the "one-liners" listed below. Phrases like these add spice to your conversation. Use the following list to help you take your conversational skills to the next level.

English	Español	Guide
Are you sure	¿Está seguro? (a)	es-**TA** say-**GOO**-row
Excellent	¡Excelente!	x-say-**LENT**-tay
Fantastic	¡Fantástico!	fan-**TA**-stee-co
Good idea	Buena idea.	boo-**A**-na e-**DAY**-ah

English	Español	Guide
Happy birthday	¡Feliz cumpleaños!	fay-LEASE coom-play-AH-nyos
Have a nice day	Tenga un buen día.	TEN-ga un boo-WAYNE D-ah
I agree	De acuerdo.	day ah-coo-AIR-doe
I believe so	Creo que sí.	**CRAY**-oh kay **SEE**
I'm so glad	Me alegro.	may ah-**LAY**-gro
I'll be right back	¡Ahora vengo!	ah-**OR**-ah **VEIN**-go
I'm leaving now	¡Ya me voy!	ya may **VOY**
That's OK	Está bien.	es-**TA** b-**N**
It's important	Es importante.	es eem-pour-**TAHN**-tay
It's serious	Es grave.	es **GRA**-vay
It's possible	Es posible	es po-**SEE**-blay
Like this	¿Así?	ah-**SEE**
Maybe.	Quizás.	key-**SAHS**
Me, neither	Yo tampoco.	yo tam-**PO**-co
Me, too	Yo también.	yo tam-b-**N**
More or less	Más o menos.	**MAS** oh **MAY**-nos
Really	¿De veras?	day **VER**-ahs
Sure	¡Claro!	**CLA**-row
That depends.	Depende.	day-**PEN**-day
We'll see you.	Nos vemos.	nos **VAY**-mos

Tips & Tidbits

Use short phrases to spice up your conversation. Start with one phrase per week and see how many different situations you can occur where you can use your "phrase of the week."

96

Typing in Spanish on Your Computer
Inserting Letters with Shortcut Keys

When you need to type letters with accent marks or use Spanish punctuation, you will use keys that you have probably never used before! Actually, you are *composing characters* using the **control** key. It is located on the bottom row of keys. You will see that it is such an important key that there is one on both sides. It keeps the computer from moving forward one space so that the accent goes on *top* of the letter instead of *beside* it.

Always remember to hold the control key down first. It will be the *key* to your success in word processing Spanish. With a little practice these keys will become a normal part of your word processing skills.

Also, if using MS Word, you may use the menu command Insert>Symbol.

To insert	For a PC, Press	For a Mac, Press
á, é, í, ó, ú, ý Á, É, Í, Ó, Ú, Ý	CTRL+' (APOSTROPHE), *the letter*	OPTION + e, *the letter*
â, ê, î, ô, û Â, Ê, Î, Ô, Û	CTRL+SHIFT+^ (CARET), *the letter*	OPTION + i, *the letter*
ã, ñ, õ Ã, Ñ, Õ	CTRL+SHIFT+~ (TILDE), *the letter*	OPTION + n, *the letter*
ä, ë, ï, ö, ü, ÿ Ä, Ë, Ï, Ö, Ü, Ÿ	CTRL+SHIFT+: (COLON), *the letter*	OPTION + u, *the letter*
¿	ALT+CTRL+SHIFT+?	OPTION+SHIFT+ ?
¡	ALT+CTRL+SHIFT+!	OPTION + !

Basic Information
Please Print

DATE: _____
       MONTH DAY YEAR

MR.
MRS.
MISS _____
FIRST NAME   MIDDLE NAME   PATERNAL SURNAME   MATERNAL SURNAME   (HUSBAND)

ADDRESS: _____
                              STREET
_____
CITY   STATE   ZIP CODE

TELEPHONE: HOME _____ WORK _____

           CELL _____ FAX _____

EMAIL ADDRESS: _____

SOCIAL SECURITY NUMBER: _____-_____-_____

NAME OF OTHER CHILDREN: _____

DATE OF BIRTH   _____
                         MONTH DAY YEAR

DRIVER'S LICENSE NUMBER: _____

OCCUPATION: _____

PLACE OF EMPLOYMENT: _____

MARITAL STATUS: MARRIED   SINGLE
                       DIVORCED   SEPARATED
                       WIDOW

HUSBAND'S NAME: _____
        FIRST NAME MIDDLE NAME PATERNAL SURNAME MATERNAL SURNAME (HUSBAND)
WIFE'S NAME: _____
        FIRST NAME MIDDLE NAME PATERNAL SURNAME MATERNAL SURNAME (HUSBAND)

IN CASE OF EMERGENCY: _____ TELEPHONE: _____

SIGNATURE: _____ DATE: _____

Practicing What You Have Learned

Practice is an important part of the language learning process. The more you include practice in your daily routine, the more comfortable and fluent you will become.

The key to practicing Spanish is to set realistic goals. Don't let the language learning process become overwhelming to you. Yes, there is a lot to learn, and it will take some time. But, by setting realistic goals, you have a greater chance of sticking with it. Each of us has different learning styles, so find out what works best for you and break the material down into small pieces. Some of us learn best by listening. Others need to write the words and phrases in order to visualize them. Generally the more of your senses that you involve in the learning process, the faster you will retain the information. Focus and practice one thing at a time. It's doing the little things that will make the greatest difference in the long run. Working five minutes every day on your Spanish is *mucho* better than trying to put in an hour of practice time only once each week. Consistency in your practice habits is vital to your success.

Here are some practice tips that have worked for me and others who have participated in *SpeakEasy's Survival Spanish*™ training programs over the last few years.

1. Start practicing first thing in the morning. The shower is a great place to start. Say the numbers or run through the months of the year while you wash your hair. If you practice when you start your day you are more likely to continue to practice as the day progresses.

2. Use your commute time to practice. Listening to CDs, music and Spanish language radio stations will help you get the rhythm of Spanish. It will also increase your vocabulary.

3. If you are stopped in traffic, look around you for numbers on billboards or the license tags of the cars in front of you to help you practice. Don't just sit there—do something!

4. Investigate sites on the internet. Sites such as www.about.spanish.com and www.studyspanish.com are great places to practice and to learn, not to mention the fact that they are free!

5. Buy Spanish magazines or pick up Spanish newspapers that are published in your area. Many magazines like *People* have Spanish versions and almost every community in the country has a Spanish language newspaper or two. Many of them are free.

6. If there aren't any Spanish newspapers in your area, you can find a variety of publications from Latin America on the internet. Major cities in Latin America all have newspapers that are easy to find on-line.

7. Practice as often as possible, even five minutes a day will help.

8. Don't give up! You didn't learn English overnight and you won't learn Spanish that way either. Set realistic goals and don't go too far too fast.

9. Learn five to ten words each week.

10. Practice at work with a friend.

11. Read! These books will make great additions to your library.

    Baez, Francia and Chong, Nilda. *Latino Culture.* Intercultural Press, 2005

    Einsohn, Marc and Steil, Gail. *The Idiot's Guide to Learning Spanish on Your Own.* Alpha Books, 1996

    Hawson, Steven R. *Learn Spanish the Lazy Way.* Alpha Books, 1999.

    Reid, Elizabeth. Spanish *Lingo for the Savvy Gringo.* In One Ear Publications, 1997

    Wald, Susana. *Spanish for Dummies.* Wiley Publishing, 2000.

About the Author

Myelita Melton, MA

Myelita Melton, founder of SpeakEasy Communications, remembers the first time she heard a "foreign" language." She knew from that moment what she wanted to do with her life. "Since I was always the kid in class that talked too much," Myelita says, "I figured it would be a good idea to learn more than one language—that way I could talk to a lot more people!" After high school, she studied in Mexico at the *Instituto de Filológica Hispánica* and completed both her BA and MA in French and Curriculum Design at Appalachian State University.

"Lita's" unique career includes classroom instruction and challenging corporate experience. She has won several national awards, including a prestigious *Rockefeller* scholarship. In 1994 she was named to *Who's Who Among Outstanding Americans.* Myelita's corporate experience includes owning a television production firm, working with NBC's Spanish news division, *Canal de Noticias,* and Charlotte's PBS affiliate WTVI. She continues to broadcast with WDAV, a National Public Radio affiliate near Lake Norman in North Carolina where she lives.

In 1997 Myelita started SpeakEasy Communications to offer industry-specific Spanish instruction in North Carolina. The company is now the nation's leader in Spanish training, offering thirty of *SpeakEasy's Survival Spanish*™ programs and publications to companies, associations, and colleges throughout the US.

Lita is also a member of the National Speaker's Association and the National Council for Continuing Education and Training. Many of her clients say she is the most high-energy, results-oriented speaker they have ever seen. As she travels the country speaking on cultural diversity issues in the workplace and languages, she has truly realized her dream of being able to talk to the world.

www.ingramcontent.com/pod-product-compliance
Lightning Source LLC
Chambersburg PA
CBHW081255170426
43198CB00017B/2799